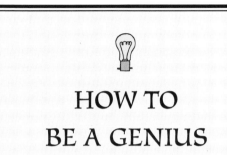

HOW TO
BE A GENIUS

$$Z_o = \frac{138}{\sqrt{Er}} \log\left(\frac{D}{d}\right)(ohms)$$

$$f_e = \frac{11.8}{\pi\left(\frac{D+d}{}\right)\sqrt{}}$$

HOW TO
BE A GENIUS

ANDRÉ DE GUILLAUME

CONTENTS

About the author

Despite being drawn in to taking part in a military coup (see page 139), test results suggest that André de Guillaume could be a bona fide genius, though he does appear to have been "on the cusp" for a while. He has successfully* pursued careers in a variety of fields (see Why I Am Not a Genius) and was specifically* chosen to write this book because of his polymathic knowledge, his commitment to the genius self-help movement, and his ability to knock out a thousand words in three and a half hours. He is currently, as mathematicians say, "working on some problems."

How to use this book

The best way to use this book is to read it. The best way to read it is to dismantle it, taking care to save the cover and the binding, and then to paste the pages in numerical order across one wall of your living room. Once you have done this you should set yourself a daily reading target and stick to it. The publishers cannot be held responsible for the consequences of any reader's failure to stick to a reading schedule. Any reader's principle aim should be to think about what he or she reads. Always.

(*Adverbs may not be accurate)

So You Want to Be a Genius?

———◆———

"One is not born a genius, one becomes a genius."

SIMONE DE BEAUVOIR

SO YOU WANT TO BE A GENIUS?

YOU WANT TO BE A GENIUS. GOOD FOR YOU. YOU COULD ALREADY BE OVER THREE-FIFTHS OF THE WAY THERE. YOU COULD BE STANDING ON THE BRINK OF FAME, FORTUNE, ALL SORTS OF OTHER BRINKS. TEST THE WATERS.

A taste for the genius life

> "Put your talent into your work, but your genius into your life." —Oscar Wilde

Who wouldn't want to be a genius? Geniuses inspire awe. They extend humanity itself. They are history's elite. They shake things up. Geniuses have outstanding and unique talents that are intellectual and often creative in some sense. (A world-beating songbird impersonator is unlikely to be recognized as a genius. Not unless he or she does something else besides.) In layman's terms, the genius thinks something new. That's what inspires the awe.

As well as deification in your field, if you're a genius, you can expect to enjoy:

- Rich and powerful people liking you*

- People hanging on your every word

- Becoming more sexually attractive

- Winning prizes on a regular basis

- Sycophants paying your bills

* Although it must be said that some might dislike you in equal measure.

Common misconceptions

There are a number of widely held ideas about genius that are just plain wrong. (If you are a genius you will obviously be able to identify and dispel these flawed ideas.) Football players are not geniuses. Golfers are not geniuses either. These truths, though self-evident, are painful for some. But they shouldn't be. The fact is geniuses love truth. They crave it. Pain and all.

Culture is relative, accumulative, and tricky. It's tempting to see sports personalities, actors, singers, and film directors as geniuses, privileging us with new emotional and psychological experiences that we didn't know we could have. But it's safer just to see them as entertainers. Entertainers can be geniuses (see chapter four), but it's rare. Geniuses from the arts need to be considered using measures of universality, longevity, and formal development. It is complicated (unless you're a genius).

Other common misconceptions

- That it's all one percent inspiration, ninety-nine percent perspiration. The greater the first percentage, the smaller the second. That's the way percentages work.

- That you have to wear a robe

- That you cannot be bald

- That you are not human

- That you have to be completely nutso

LEONARDO DA VINCI (1452–1519)—POLYMATH

- Leonardo has come to represent the archetypal Renaissance man, the polymath's polymath. He excelled at painting, engineering, aeronautics, architecture, and anatomy. His patrons included Kings Francis I and Louis XII of France, Giuliano de' Medici, and Cesare Borgia.

- Among other things, he invented the helicopter over four centuries before anyone got around to building one.

- His contribution to his teacher Andrea del Verrocchio's painting *The Baptism of Christ* marks the beginning of the Italian High Renaissance.

- He often wrote his notes in mirror writing. This may have been an attempt to keep his ideas top secret, or a method he devised as a left-hander to avoid smudging the ink.

- In 1504 he painted the *Mona Lisa*, a likeness most probably of the wife of Francesco del Giacondo, which would become the world's most famous portrait.

- Leonardo's superstar status makes him a favorite of conspiracy theorists: he's been accused of everything from faking the Turin shroud to concealing the bloodline of Christ.

Have you got what it takes?

> "Talent, lying in the understanding, is often inherited;
> genius, being the action of reason or imagination, rarely
> or never." —Samuel Taylor Coleridge

Obviously an outstanding talent is only the first requisite. It guarantees nothing. You also need stamina, grit, luck, not to die of consumption before puberty—things like that. But if you pretend those things don't count, or you can find an analytical system that allows you to discount or at least suspend their influence, then you can get yourself a checklist and start ticking boxes. Even geniuses enjoy that.

Your potential

Use these eleven steps—the test is an IQ test in that it is an Interesting Questionnaire—to assess how easy or unlikely it will be for you to become a genius. Note that this questionnaire should only be used by people over the age of four, unless in extreme genius circumstances.

Could you be a genius?

1. Do you like . . . ?
   a) Math
   b) Physics
   c) More math and more physics
   Score one point for a) and/or b). Two points for c).

2. Are you interested in . . . ?
   a) The universe
   b) Universals
   c) Golf
   One point for b), two points for a). Odd, really.

3. As a child, did you watch . . . ?
   a) Cartoons
   b) Russian cinema of the World War II
   c) The cat
   Three points for c), two for b). It just about makes
   sense if you think it through.

4. Have you ever . . . ?
   a) Found a four-leaf clover
   b) Designed a cathedral
   c) Registered an invention
   Two points for more than one of any of the above.

5. Have you ever said . . . ?
   a) "Knowledge is the precarious peak upon

which we stand to survey the world."

b) "Knowledge is the library and stuff. Right?"

c) "No ledges on my windows."

The correct answer is none of the above. Two points.

6. Rate the following statements on a scale of one to ten, one being, "no way!" and ten being, "I'm the boss, I'm the boss, I'm the boss!"
   a) "I would sacrifice my wife, my children, my home—everything for my career."
   b) "All I need to do is take Crowthorne's thesis out of Professor Lodge's pigeonhole and replace it with my own."
   c) "I really, really like math."

   If you rate any of the statements at more than five, your potential just won another two points.

7. Which are you, generally . . . ?
   a) Yes
   b) No
   c) Maybe

   Not surprisingly, "no" gets nothing. Otherwise, bag the numbers: one for a), two for c).

8. You feel most comfortable in:
   a) The lab
   b) A dusty university study
   c) A franchised coffee bar

   Owing to contractual obligations, a) and b) get you two points, c) gets you four. And remember, genius loves a cappuccino to go!

9. The previous eight questions have been patronizing and have failed to engage my intellect.
   a) Agree
   b) Disagree
   c) Feel emptiness and ennui
   No points for disagreeing. Otherwise, help yourself.

10. Which statement comes closest to tinkering with your brain waves?
    a) "Physical exercise helps me focus my thinking."
    b) "Physical exercise makes me look fit and thus more attractive to the opposite sex."
    c) "Physical exercise? No way!"
    A point for each one. Potentially three points.

11. Final thoughts?
    a) OK
    b) Yep
    c) Cappuccino?
    Yes, c) gets the points.

So, check your score. Lots of points is good. Not many is bad. And anything in between is, well . . . in between.

As a genius, you should, by now, have realized that the questionnaire is as meaningless as meaningless can be. It is merely a way of making you think about your own life and its potential for genius.

Methods for improving your brain power

You've got potential. You're on your way. But an outstanding intellect, like any muscle, requires regular exercise. You need to get yourself some strategies that keep your brilliant mind at its brightest and best. That dazzling brain of yours needs constant polishing.

The following tips are some tried-and-true methods for getting your cognitive cogs a-turning. Using them can only do you good.

- Whenever making a cash transaction, try to work out the change in your head before the electronic register does.

- Whenever you are walking along an urban street, try to estimate the number of parked cars and the length of the street. You will be able to calculate the average space taken up by each vehicle and you can work out the street's maximum parking capacity. You could decide on a minimum distance necessary between each car and introduce that factor into the equation. Be careful not to get run over—that hampers your chances of achieving the exalted status you seek.

- Think outside boxes, envelopes, and other containers. Try to make unusual conceptual concordances. What happens if you strap a mouse to a tennis ball? What if you teach a snake to play the guitar? This helps you to develop new ideas and new inspirations. Can an electric eel power a microwave for four minutes?

- Get a notepad and write the word "IDEAS" on the front. If you're right-handed do it with your left hand and vice versa. That way it will look childish and historians will think you had your ideas in your prodigious youth.

- Memorize things. Your super-brain needs as much information to crunch on as it can get. Feed it. (See chapter six for more on this.)

- Read complicated books. This is one of the basic strands of genius training. You need to know what everyone else has thought in order to make sure your idea is original.

- Try thinking in new ways: numbers, shapes, colors, metaphors. The ability to think differently is an important and useful skill.

AVOIDABLE BEHAVIOR

Avoid the following traits if you are going to make the most of things.

- **Laziness.** Laziness is all right in some ways. But even if you are draped across a chaise longue, out of your mind on the finest Chinese opium, you should always be mentally focused on your current project.

- **Stupidity.** There is no way around it—genius is not stupid. If you find yourself being stupid, snap out of it by thinking something complex.

- **Ideological Commitment.** If you nail your colors to a mast, you may find your ship sinking. A genius believes in the truth. That's all there is.

- **Addiction.** A genius is almost as vulnerable to addiction as regular folk. All those potential geniuses that never made it because addiction got them—we don't even know their names.

- **Commercialism.** Do not do it for the cash. You might make lots of money, and good luck to you if you do. But it shouldn't be your motivation. It simply won't work.

- **Boredom.** After childhood, when it's OK, boredom must not be tolerated. It should function only as a fleeting reminder that things need to be done. Those with super-brains ought to use them.

- **Jokes.** Know any good philosopher jokes? Exactly.

- **Violence.** There are always exceptions. In general though, "live by the sword, die by the sword" is a tad extreme for your average particle physicist.

- **Hobbies.** Once you're world-renowned, get a train set by all means. Aspiring geniuses don't have the time.

CHAPTER ONE

The Pros and Cons
of a Genius Lifestyle

"Innovators and men of genius have almost
always been regarded as fools at the
beginning (and very often at the end)
of their careers."

FYODOR DOSTOYEVSKY

THE PROS AND CONS
OF A GENIUS LIFESTYLE

BEING A GENIUS SERIOUSLY AFFECTS YOUR LIFE. INDEED, IT BECOMES YOUR LIFE. SO YOU NEED TO ASSESS THE BALANCE OF ADVANTAGES AND DISADVANTAGES IF YOU'RE THINKING OF DOING SOME GENUINE ENVELOPE-PUSHING.

The fruits of genius

It might seem that being a genius is a golden ticket to a life of glamorous soirees with the intellectual elite, champagne flute in hand, arm candy at your side, surrounded by a throng of smiling sycophants. But you might be confusing this scene with the lifestyle of a diplomat. Get your expectations right from the start. First, let's consider the many advantages.

Status

Genius is the ultimate in status. You can be a great; you can be a colossus; you can be a legend. As a genius, you also have mystery. The whole point is that nobody has access to some truth about the world in the way you do. People are bound to gaze at you in awestruck amazement. This can be satisfying. Geniuses *are* godlike—above mundane human experience. Most importantly, they think the new thought for us. And this is the most precious of gifts. Newton showed everybody that the universe is like some big mechanical toy, and he had the math to prove it. He got to be Master of the Mint and President of the Royal Society. Yes, the genius's gift changes the world for us. So they get R-E-S-P-E-C-T.

Social space

What can you do with respect? For the godlike intellect, there is available a whole impressionist's palette of exclusion from social regulations. You certainly shouldn't feel you need to behave or appear as an ordinary mortal would.

Fashion statement

Pianist Glenn Gould was always worried about being cold. Even when it wasn't cold. So he wore big overcoats and hats when he gave concerts. Einstein sometimes didn't wear socks. You can exclude yourself from convention because you have higher concerns. And it's OK.

"I'm with the genius"

When it comes to behavior, knock yourself out! The situation is helped by other people's expectations and allowances. "He's Bertrand Russell, I *had* to sleep with him!" sounds like a reasonable sentiment. The same can be said for, "*Of course* he twitches as though he had no control over his body. He's Samuel Johnson, the inventor of the dictionary!"

Make a name for yourself

Get your name attached to something. The Pythagorean theorem, or the Möbius strip—something catchy like that. Ideally, you should be looking for a neat, universal law to be named after you. You may not be familiar with *On the Electrodynamics of Moving Bodies*, but you've probably heard of $E=mc^2$. You may be vaguely aware that a body immersed in a fluid is buoyed up by a force equal to the weight of the displaced fluid, but you're more likely to have heard of Archimedes's principle.

The genius's name becomes synonymous with his or her ideas—consider Darwin, Newton, Curie. Yes, the genius's *name*. Because that's what will live forever—your name and your idea, of course, but not you. It's a *kind* of living forever. But not one that you can experience. And anyway, what is "forever?"

With any luck you could get a decade or two of solid fame and adulation. This should make it worth the effort. Everyone knows who you are, you can put your sartorial and social inadequacy plans into action, and you can really live the life of the super-being.

Feel-good factor

Then, of course, there's that good old-fashioned smug self-satisfaction. That idea you had—your dazzling thought—you were right! And now the whole world sees the whole world in a different light, a light that shines your name upon the heavens. Or, maybe the world just gets to see triangles from a fresh perspective; the point's the same. Humanity's understanding of the many mysteries of its own experience has moved one step further along the long highway of enlightenment. Thanks to you. Give yourself a pat on the back. Everyone else is doing it.

ISAAC NEWTON (1642–1727)
—PHYSICIST, ASTRONOMER, MATHEMATICIAN

- The son of a Lincolnshire, English, farmer, Newton went to Trinity College Cambridge. He went on to become a fellow there and was made a professor in 1669.

- Interested in optics—to the extent that he once stuck a spike in his eye socket to see what would happen—Newton invented the reflecting telescope, a vast improvement on the existing single-lens telescope.

- His genius work, *Philosophiae Naturalis Principia Mathematica*, was published in 1687. It introduced the laws of motion and universal gravity.

- There were problems of attribution for Newton, and he became involved in a dispute with Gottfried Leibniz over the discovery of differential calculus. According to their peers, they both invented it simultaneously.

- Knighted by Queen Anne in 1705 (for his work at the royal mint rather than any scientific achievement), Newton was deservedly buried in Westminster Abbey.

- Poet Alexander Pope treated Newton's legacy with greater respect. He composed the famous epitaph: "Nature and nature's laws lay hid in night / God said, 'Let Newton be' and all was light."

But now the down side . . .

If the advantages haven't put you off, consider the disadvantages. The whole of this chapter is one great big elastic equation. In a way.

Prepare to be a loner

The genius lifestyle often involves a lot of time spent alone. This is because of the thinking time required and the practicalities of writing the play or the opera or the calculations. Not only is it lonely at the top, it's lonely on the way there too. You will have to shun friends, destroy enemies, develop a ruthless streak.

Cut off from social interaction, your quest to formulate your ideas may consume and destroy you; your brilliance may fade into silence. Philosopher Immanuel Kant seemed not to have thought anything for at least a decade in the late 1700s and it looked for a while as though he had lost it. But he came back strongly with the dazzlingly clever *Critique of Pure Reason* and sealed his reputation. If you can take the knock to your social life, the isolation will pay off in the end.

There ain't no sanity clause

Genius can make you go mad. The reason is what's technically called "brain burn." This is a condition that can affect geniuses from time to time. Usually it goes away with a bit of bed rest or some electric shock therapy or trepanning. If they do zap the juice out of you and you're already established as a genius, they won't want to keep you and you'll be able to go home and blabber like an imbecile there. That's the happier option.

And sometimes your genius itself can be downright depressing. You may not have discovered a wacky new chemical that everyone finds amusing; you may have revealed an unpalatable truth about our lives or our world. Your genius might be to discover exactly how our world is about to meet its imminent doom. Don't expect your research project to be a barrel of laughs.

You mean he was a genius after all?

To be avoided at all costs is posthumous recognition. Depending on your point of view, this is either really bad luck or the gods taking it out on you with a vengeance.

Often it's not quite so severe—if you're a Shakespeare or a Mozart or a Caravaggio, you do get plenty of recognition during your lifetime. It's just that your contemporaries, clever though they obviously must be, might not appreciate just how special your talent is. You could, however, end up in the poorhouse, or out of favor, lonely, bankrupt, and forced to sell all your stuff like Rembrandt. The bottom line is that you may end your life not knowing if posterity will bestow its blessing.

Be optimistic, though. You know you're right. They'll realize in time.

Cultivate the genius lifestyle

Test the boundaries of style slowly: egg on your tie one week, sweater on backward the next. But try to be original. Too many people just go for lab coat and sneakers. Bor-ing.

1. Whatever your style decisions, remember to wash. No one wants to bestow a Nobel Prize on a smelly scruff.
2. Be modest in the presence of presidents and kings—they're just not clever enough to understand why you're greater than they are.
3. Make sure your name sticks to the idea. This is best achieved by staying alive as long as possible. Had Charles Darwin fallen under a bus before he published, the name Alfred Russel Wallace would undoubtedly be attached to the idea of natural selection today.
4. The journey from isolated study to brightly lit social whirl can be quick and startling. But do try to remember the important names—princes, presidents, prime ministers, popes.
5. Your genius may well attract power. Be careful. For the artistic or scientific genius, politics is a dangerous arena. Or you may know more physics than anyone alive, but politicians don't play by rules.
6. If you want to use your ideas to make money, don't be afraid to be a self-publicist. It doesn't hurt Stephen Hawking's profile to appear on *The Simpsons*.
7. If you are an artistic genius, hang on to the money. You will, of course, make a comeback, but you might not be alive to see it.
8. Make sure you go out sometimes. A brisk walk is good for you.
9. Finally, all the other tips are eclipsed by "the idea." Pursue "the idea" at all costs.

A SUMMARY OF THE PROS/CONS

The public will adore and worship you unfalteringly.

Your peers will resent and undermine you. Unfalteringly.

People always think of you when they draw triangles. You reveal a fundamental truth. About triangles.

People know nothing about you, except that once you said something about triangles.

You can behave as though you are totally crazy.

Your fundamental truth is not popular.

You can behave as though you are totally and completely crazy.

You might actually be totally and completely mad.

Your name lives forever and stretches into eternity.

You do not actually get to live forever. Much as you may want to.

CHAPTER TWO

Early Signs of Genius

———•◆•———

"The reluctance to put away childish things
may be a requirement of genius."

REBECCA PEPPER SINKLER

EARLY SIGNS OF GENIUS

NOT ONE HUNDRED PERCENT SURE YOU ACTUALLY ARE A GENIUS? THERE ARE SIGNS. STUDY THEM. YOU SHOULD AT LEAST BE GOOD AT THAT SORT OF THING—INTERPRETING AND SUCHLIKE.

The prodigy and the slow starter

Lots of geniuses have been prodigies. So prodigious behavior is definitely something to look for. Some good questions to ask yourself: How many operas have I written? Did I stand in the library with my hands at my sides discoursing with the university lecturers from my father's college when I was only six? Were my teenage years spent in the shed making gadgets and explosions? Is my dad away laying siege to Byzantium? If your answers are five, yes, yes, and yes, respectively, you're already close.

Another excellent indicator of the early promise of great greatness is the "astounding feat." The astounding feat is something that sets the prodigy apart from his or her peers. This might be something like publishing a novel or writing a symphony while still in your teens, but a good sign generally is surpassing the abilities of your teachers.

If you're not a prodigy you needn't worry, you can still be a genius. In fact, even if you majored in mediocrity until your thirties, if you really lay claim to the title with a world-shaking idea or invention, biographers will mythologize your past until it turns out that you had been able, after all, to recite pi to 50 decimal points when you were only four. But it helps if you give them some material to work with.

WOLFGANG AMADEUS MOZART (1756–1791) —COMPOSER

- The son of Leopold, deputy Kapellmeister to the court orchestra of the Archbishop of Salzburg, Mozart made his first professional European tour aged six.

- The "Amadeus" part of his name is the Latinized version of one of the names that appears on his birth certificate: Theophilis.

- In 1782 he married Constanze Weber against the wishes of his father. She was a good wife and bore him six children, but she couldn't manage her husband's spending. Mozart was in debt when he died and was buried in a communal grave in Vienna.

- Joseph Haydn was one of Mozart's close friends. Haydn called him the greatest composer he knew. The two played music together and were even members of the same lodge of Freemasons. Mozart's opera *Die Zauberflöte* (*The Magic Flute*) is said to contain Masonic symbols and ideas.

- Mozart wrote 15 masses, more than 50 symphonies, 21 piano concertos, and 21 stage or operatic works.

- Two popular myths, fed by Peter Shaffer's play and subsequent film, *Amadeus*, are that Mozart was poisoned by his colleague Antonio Salieri, and that he felt that he was writing his final requiem for himself, rather than Count Walsegg, the man who commissioned it.

What it means if you love equations

You're eight years old. It's a Sunday and it's raining. You are watching the raindrops streaking down the outside of the windows. Something occurs to you about the number of streaks and the speeds at which they run. You see an idea in your mind—not in words or symbols, but in shapes and absences—that makes you feel that the idea has some fundamental truth. You realize soon afterward that mathematical ideas slot simply into your mind, and the relationships between them seem immediately clear. You are thinking about complicated ideas and it makes you feel good. You are on your way.

Fostering good obsession

Thinking about complicated ideas is something that geniuses have in common and do a lot. When most people think about complicated things they get a headache or get angry or drunk. The fact that your fizzy imagination enjoys complexity gives you an edge. This pleasure, while helpful in keeping you hardworking and dogged, can edge itself into obsession. One risk with which the genius frequently struggles is that his or her field of excellence will become an escape from real life, with all its vicissitudes. Clinically, there are two kinds of obsession: good obsession and bad obsession. Good obsession keeps you motivated and curious; bad obsession destroys you and those around you. The choice may or may not be yours.

Falling in love with quadratics

To most people algebra and equations are boring things that math teachers make you do in order to ruin your teenage years. But then it lies beyond most people to understand the unfailing gorgeousness of an equals sign, the jaunty knowingness of brackets, or the universal mystery that is x^2. These algebraic icons give the youthful math prodigy a way of seeing the world as meaningful and balanced. Equations are not only examples of sparkling perfection in a world chock-full of ugliness and decay; they also last. So if you are a budding numbers genius, look for a snappy equation to help your name endure.

Eccentricity as standard

One of the best things about being a genius is that people expect, and therefore are more prepared to tolerate, a certain eccentricity of behavior. You can deliver lectures wearing your slippers, become catatonic during a dinner party, be socially incompetent, or even go nuts. Experiment.

Your great mind has a different way of seeing and the great masses know this. Often the more batty behavior you exhibit, the more adulation you'll receive. As a genius, you're like a seer, or perhaps a shaman. Your role is to act as if there is a higher knowledge, another reality. Which, of course, there is. Your genius reassures the masses of exactly that fact.

Keeping out of a straitjacket

There is, however, a downside to the bonanza of quirky tics that is you. The man in the street also half-expects that your weird lifestyle might, at times, necessitate the odd spell in a straightjacket, holed up in the padded suite of a gothic Victorian asylum. Your wackiness might be interpreted in the light of the idea that there is a thin line between genius and madness. And you may, on reflection, find that you actually are mad. In which case you shouldn't be too surprised by the odd spell in the bouncy dungeon. The problem is that your thinking has to border on the edges of reason, and hanging out on the borders of reason takes its toll.

Part of your social inadequacy may stem from your over-treading the path of the solitary individual. The hours of free-associating and zapping neural connections while walking in the lonely hills above the town make you a stranger to the rules of conversational dynamics and liable to be too spontaneous, blurting out something painfully immature or petulant. Take into account, though, that lots and lots of people are strangers to the rules of conversational dynamics and are forever blurting out some nonsense. So don't worry too much. Social frigidity or flammability is really only part of a larger scheme of very odd behavior.

Think of a way to be eccentric and endearing. That's the most popular combination. It can be as easy as always wearing the same dilapidated cardigan every day or calling everybody "mysterious bard." It seems like a little thing, but biographers love this kind of individual touch.

FIVE WAYS TO REACH ECCENTRIC BEHAVIOR

- Spend as much time as you can thinking

- Say everything that comes into your head

- Keep notes on everything

- Hardly ever finish anything

- Spend as much time as possible alone

Who's your daddy?

Parentage is often important for the genius. Essentially you should be looking for something a little bit different. Perhaps your father was a noble and your mother a peasant girl. Perhaps you had a gypsy uncle who would play the violin at family events and encouraged your love of anthropology. Perhaps you were raised at court and personally tutored by a Greek philosopher. All are good signs and bode well.

Your loss is your gain

There are some general points to factor in when considering your childhood. It helps if your parents are emotionally flawed or absent or alcoholic or dead. You need something to give you an early sense of loss or grief or yearning. If your mother dies in childbirth or your father dies before you're born, that helps too.

Like it or not, some good psychological scarring will pay dividends in the long run. The mechanism by which these dividends will be realized is that the youthful prodigy enters a world of emotional and intellectual loneliness and isolation. (According to most health professionals, loneliness and isolation should be taken only in moderation, but short bursts can free the imagination from the interference of things like friendships, romances, and that old chestnut: the dead hand of social conformity.)

Being a loner does, of course, have risks. Some loners do not in fact become geniuses—they become psychopaths. Psychopathology should be discouraged.

Family structure? An adoptee, an orphan, an only child, one of 12, over-loved by the father, neglected by the father, neglected by both parents, neglected by both parents and all of your 11 siblings (until that one day at breakfast, on your 10th birthday, when you spoke and they all suddenly realized). Whatever the scenario, it doesn't matter much. Any family combination has possibility. As ever, isolation and some form of childhood neglect or trauma usually helps.

School is overrated

Unless you're being apprenticed to a Florentine painter, school is often not that important. Being educated at home and alone by a brilliant parent or some pedagogic guardian can accelerate the learning process, thus giving you intellectual superiority over your childhood peers (should you meet any) and encouraging you to think that life is about hard work. It should also ensure that you have problems socializing. Remember that whether they're strapping you to a violin at the age of four or farming you out to a crazy aunt for your formative years, your folks are just doing their bit to help you along Genius Avenue.

The genius gender

Throughout human history women have risen to the top when allowed. It's the "when allowed" bit that's been the *problème femme* in the genius world rankings. If we look, we can see plentiful evidence of female achievement. Consider the work of Sofonisba Anguissola (court painter for Philip II, remember?), or the brilliance of a Clara Peeters still life (which I'm sure you've seen at least once on a postcard).

Long odds

Too often patriarchal cultures have forbidden or discouraged the participation of women. Just look at the case of Clara Schumann: pianist, composer, and wife of Robert Schumann. In fact, let Clara speak for herself. One minute she's like, "There is nothing that surpasses the joy of creation," and then she's all like, "A woman must not desire to compose." If you are a woman and considering the path of genius, you will need extra reserves of determination to weather the rainy Monday morning of patronizing assumptions and sexist bigotry*.

The odds against a man becoming a genius are 1:238 million. The odds against a woman becoming a genius are 1: 812 million. As Pythagoras once said, "Do the math."

---

* Another possible route for aspiring women is known as the "power behind the throne" scenario. It's sort of genius by proxy. You will need a powerful and intelligent man lacking in imagination. A buyers' market.

Your hidden pedigree

The following background checklist will allow you to assess the promising mulch of your developmental years. It should be interpreted metaphorically, symbolically, and loosely. Look for the good in people, including yourself, and excepting professional rivals.

Are you a genius in the making?

1. You have a degree from:
    a) The Sorbonne
    b) The Academy at Athens
    c) The Internet

2. Your hobby is:
    a) Playing Internet chess against a super-computer
    b) Composing verse epics using a language that you invented
    c) Playstation

3. At your birth, the midwife said:
    a) "A boy!"
    b) "What is that?"
    c) "Oh, it's a girl. Never mind, Mrs Einstein."

4. Your childhood best friend was:
    a) Imaginary
    b) Your mother
    c) Douglas from next door

5. Your favorite music is:
    a) A quintet for strings that you wrote when you were 12
    b) John Cage's silence thing
    c) Abba

6. Your father says things like:
    a) "The pope has summoned me to Rome."
    b) "You are a beam of light, my child, a beam of light."
    c) "I didn't get laundry detergent because it wasn't on the list."

7. Your guinea pig was called:
    a) Euclid
    b) x^2
    c) Mister Guinea Pig

8. Your earliest ambition was to be:
    a) A train driver
    b) Immortal
    c) Driving a BMW by the age of 21

If you scored mostly a)s or b)s, you might be genius material. If you got mostly c)s, focus on developing your eccentric side to compensate. It's your only chance.

TOP FIVE JUNIOR ACHIEVERS

- **Wolfgang Amadeus Mozart.** Dad-tutored, little Wolfie was a precocious tot. A veteran performer by the age of eight, he was always bound for greatness.

- **Blaise Pascal.** Dad-tutored, and frequently surrounded by philosophers, he was a sure thing to start dashing off treatises in his teens.

- **Pablo Picasso.** Dad-tutored, a veritable painting infant, he was never really destined to finish school.

- **Leonardo da Vinci.** At least Da Vinci was farmed out by his dad. But again, the teenage apprentice soon outshines his master.

- **William Sidis.** Aged 11, he delivered a talk on "four-dimensional bodies" to the bigwigs at the Harvard Mathematical Club. Always a bit shy, he became something of a recluse.

CHAPTER THREE

A Brief History of Genius

"If you would understand anything, observe
its beginning and its development."

ARISTOTLE

A BRIEF HISTORY OF GENIUS

AS AN ADVANCED APE, YOU ARE A PRODUCT OF YOUR GENES; BUT, INTELLECTUALLY, YOU ARE A PRODUCT OF YOUR ENVIRONMENT. YOUR ENVIRONMENT NEEDS TO BE INTELLECTUALLY DYNAMIC. THIS WILL REQUIRE SOME LUCK. FOR EXAMPLE PHILOSOPHY, MATH, CULTURE, AND THINKING IN GENERAL WERE BIG WITH THE ANCIENT GREEKS, BIG WITH EARLY ISLAM, BUT NOT SO BIG WITH THE MEDIEVAL CHRISTIAN CHURCH.

The philosophy whiz kids

Want to know how it all got started? Let's take our minds back to another age. An age pre- almost everything. An age in need of something to talk about. Step up, Heraclites, Pythagoras, Socrates, Plato, Aristotle, Aeschylus, Aristophanes, Euripides, Sophocles, Homer. A top squad. They gave us philosophy, poetry, drama, some mathematics, politics—you know, "culture." They may have inherited some of their ideas from other civilizations, but why complicate things? What they wrote down and passed on was a conviction that proof was key to knowing stuff. Rational deduction was the way forward. Still sounds fresh, doesn't it? It's also another magical key to the state of genius—you will need to prove it.

Socratic method

Socrates liked to ask lots of questions as a way of getting to truths. Looking for contradictions and agreements and suchlike. Hardly seems like a big deal now, but it started ethics as a field of inquiry and got philosophy in general off to a strong start.

Ask too many questions, though, and they might get fed up with you and make you drink hemlock, like what happened to poor old Socrates. Whatever your field of conceptual toil, remember that ideas can be dangerous, they can upset people, and their value may go down as well as up.

The cluster

Think about it: Socrates teaches Plato. Plato sets up the Academy, the world's first philosophy department, and teaches Aristotle. Aristotle teaches some boy who later becomes Alexander the Great. OK, so Alexander didn't go into teaching, but this bunch of classical brainiacs makes a good case for the idea of an early genius hot spot in the Mediterranean.

Too busy watching gladiators

For some reason Roman philosophers just didn't do it like the Greeks. Roman philosophers did exist but they just didn't reach the peaks. Then Christianity settled in Europe and philosophy stars as Sleeping Beauty for hundreds of years. In the Middle East a brand-new religion, Islam, gives philosophy a home. Someone had to keep that learning-and-proving bug alive.

The old days are back

Thank God for the Renaissance? No, thank Aristotle and the boys from Greece and Rome, back in fashion again after more than a millennium. It's time for a whole new cornucopia of philosophers with crazy and memorable names: Copernicus, Machiavelli, Erasmus, Montaigne, Descartes, Spinoza.

And on it went, a veritable Enlightenment—Kant, Hegel, Marx, Nietzsche. A whole bucketful of world-class thinking. Philosophy, once again, laying claim to the home of genius.

The math gurus

This time we can start with the Babylonians, the Egyptians, and the Sumerians. They sort of developed geometry. It helped with agriculture and building. But, again, it was the Greeks who picked the ball up and ran with it. In much the same way that James Brown is known as the Godfather of Soul, Euclid is known as the Godfather of Geometry for his math book, *Elements*. Euclid got it written down so that we can read it today. Which leads to another principle of genius development: genius needs to be recorded if it is going to survive.

What's it made of?

Science, like math, is complicated. The history of science is complicated too. Chemistry, physics, and biology do turn up in ancient history, but not in a way we would recognize. Certainly, pre-scientific cultures liked tin, lead, gold, copper, and bronze, so there was a bit of basic chemistry going on. But as with geometry, a particular group of people wanted to get systematic about things. Empedocles came up with the idea that all matter is made of elements. Brilliant! But he decided they were earth, wind, fire, and water. Interesting—and popular with pagans still—but not quite so brilliant. A bit of a wild guess, really. Democritus thought that all matter was made of particles ("*atomos*"), which turned out to be another top-shelf idea. Even it was not really developed for a couple of millennia.

Middle age crisis

In the Middle Ages, science is all about alchemy and gunpowder. (This trend—science as a means of making wealth or war—is, of course, still with us today.) There is a real need for genius to come along and point out that alchemy is a load of garbage. But the process is gradual. The Renaissance gives birth slowly to the Enlightenment. The process involves various be-wigged, be-ruffed, and bewildered, eccentric aristocrat-types noting that different stuff has different properties and that perhaps you could analyze and group "elements" according to these properties. Then various wacky guys use "experiments" to "invent" various wacky chemicals. Hydrogen and oxygen are "discovered." It's all a bit chaotic and piecemeal. And a good time for geniuses.

Perhaps the biggest name in chemistry, Dmitry Mendeleyev, is so big because he finally sorted out those elements with his periodic table—named, possibly, after a kitchen table on which he periodically worked. In 1869, his table and its magic key—atomic weight—organized the elements that Empedocles had had a brainwave about all those centuries ago. Mendeleyev crosses the finish line first, winks roguishly at the crowd, and collects his genius badge.

STEPHEN HAWKING (1942–)—PHYSICIST

- Hawking started studying mathematics at University College, Oxford, before switching to physics because he thought it would be more interesting. Later, after beginning a postgraduate course in astronomy at Oxford, Hawking changed subjects and universities, deciding that theoretical cosmology at Cambridge would be more interesting.

- Amyotrophic lateral sclerosis, a form of motor neuron disease also referred to as Lou Gehrig's disease, struck Hawking when he was 21. He was given only a few years to live. Although the illness made him severely disabled, he is still alive and working.

- *A Brief History of Time* is Hawking's best-known book. First published in 1988, it has sold over nine million copies.

- In 1975, Kip Thorne from the California Institute of Technology had a bet with Hawking about the existence of black holes: If they were proved to exist, Thorne would get a year's subscription to *Penthouse*. If they were proved not to exist, Hawking would get four years' subscription to *Private Eye*. Hawking has conceded defeat.

- In a 1993 episode of *Star Trek*, Hawking appeared as himself.

The modern genius

The modern genius is exemplified by none other than Stephen Hawking. He's modern because he's computerized and techno. And yet he's also science fiction, which makes him a sort of paranormal fictional character. It's definitely a tough act to follow. You would have to do something like establish yourself as a genius and then clone yourself and then you could grow up to be another genius and so on and so forth. But you should really have realized by now that it doesn't work like that.

History test

1. According to Henry Ford, history is:
   a) Junk
   b) Drunk
   c) Bunk
   d) Funk

2. Philosophy started in:
   a) 455 B.C.E.
   b) 555 B.C.E.
   c) 2000 B.C.E.
   d) Cavemen's heads

3. The term "renaissance" means:
   a) Re-arrangement

b) Rebirth

c) Re-design

d) Re-mortgage

4. Oscar Wilde famously told a customs officer that he had nothing to declare but his . . .

   a) Genius

   b) Platypus

   c) Pajama tops

   d) Suitcase of booze and smokes

5. Phrenology is the now obsolete science of determining personality by means of:

   a) A friendly questionnaire

   b) Head bumps

   c) Talking over a beer

   d) Embalming in wax

6. Finish Karl Marx's catchphrase: "History repeats itself, first as tragedy, second as . . . "

   a) Farce

   b) Slapstick

   c) Documentary

   d) Live album

The answers are available by reading history.

THE OLD SCHOOL

- **Socrates.** One of history's greatest and best-known philosophers, he never wrote anything down. That's confidence.

- **Plato.** A fine example to any aspiring genius, Plato's move from wrestling to political philosophy was a majestical leap of faith.

- **Aristotle.** Well traveled and influential though he may have been, Aristotle failed to notice that whales are mammals.

- **Pythagoras.** Imagine being bound for all human history to a right-angled triangle. Have some sympathy for poor Pythagoras.

- **Aeschylus.** Although virtually responsible for inventing drama as we know it, this couldn't save Aeschylus from a hideously quirky death. An eagle dropped a tortoise on his bald head, thinking it was a stone. The blow killed him.

- **Aristophanes.** This Greek showed, amazingly enough, that you can write a play called *The Frogs* and still be a genius.

- **Euripides.** In order to take drama forward, Euripides made his plays funny and sad. In a very old-fashioned way, he was a bit modern.

- **Sophocles.** Sophocles was the top Greek playwright. He won more first prizes than anybody else. And he also gave the world, via Dr. Sigmund Freud, the ever-disturbing idea that men might desire their mothers.

- **Heraclites.** Only fragments of his work still exist, and he wrote in riddles— the perfect foundation for a lasting reputation.

- **Homer.** It may be that Homer didn't exist as a single person. He does now.

CHAPTER FOUR

Fields of Genius

—————•·•—————

"Philosophy becomes poetry and science
imagination, in the enthusiasm of genius."

BENJAMIN DISRAELI

FIELDS OF GENIUS

SO WHERE SHOULD YOU INVEST YOUR GARGANTUAN INTELLECT? IT'S CERTAINLY A PROBABLE CASE TO SPECULATE THAT SOME FIELDS OF UNDERSTANDING ARE BIGGER HITTERS THAN OTHERS. TRY SOME OF THESE ON FOR SIZE.

Can you prove you exist?

Philosophy makes a nice claim for being the original site of thinking new ideas. You can hear the teacher in the first lesson of your first philosophy class: "Everything is philosophy; philosophy is everything." (The psychology guy is saying something similar in the next classroom.)

Philosophy is odd. It's like the ultimate intellectual pursuit, yet who knows any philosophy? Who knows a philosopher? The media yell at you about the human genome project or robots on Mars, but when do they ever say anything about the current state of national philosophy? Philosophy may be in one of its periodic states of flux, presently waning a bit. Certainly not to be counted out, though.

Cold and calculating?

Again, getting your name on something is what counts—and counting may be important to you. The Pythagorean theorem may not have been the Pythagorean theorem. But it doesn't matter now. Pythagoras is the man. That's the way it goes with math geniuses. You need something to attach to your name so you can be remembered. We know that Möbius had a strip and Pascal a triangle. Their ideas are way too complicated for most of us, so we need something that we understand. If you are a math super-mind, get a rhombus, or a dodecahedron. Make it yours. Or else maybe you could try computing.

Baffle them

Mathematical paradoxes are a good, solid way of getting your name some currency. You don't even need to give people an idea they can use, more a problem that someone will have to resolve further down the long bumpy road of discovery. Zeno's paradoxes about motion and distance worked for him for centuries and can still get people scratching their heads today. Even greats like Aristotle and Leonardo felt the need to have a paradox. Aristotle has Aristotle's wheel paradox, which even manages a little bit of mystery.

Whatever happened to that old chemistry set?

Chemistry, a growth area in the Enlightenment, now seems a bit tired. There are, however, still openings for the ambitious genius who feels comfortable around Bunsen burners and flasks. If you're looking to be a genius in the next generation or so, chemistry looks a good bet if you've got a gold-plated, copper-bottomed solution to global warming. A solution where we all still get to stay alive.

Let's get physical

One field of inquiry where genius is currently a-happenin' is physics. Physics has produced some first-class examples. Genius is a term never uncertainly applied to Isaac Newton or Albert Einstein—two figures who walk in the truly godlike upper echelons of the G-word's spatial metaphor for hierarchy. And they are godlike because they looked over the fence at God's greenhouse—the heavens. They figured it all out with some dazzling brain work and told us that either God wasn't up there, or his plan was way crazier than anyone had thought. Big stuff.

Physics gives us the modern world, the nuclear age, the big bang, photons, electrons, quarks—all those things that we don't understand but know explain an awful lot. Physics is apparently on the lookout for a "unified theory" that will "explain everything." It's there for the taking—your name attached to the explanation of everything. It would look great on your resume, get you into all sorts of exclusive parties, and onto all sorts of exclusive committees.

Problem-solving

Of course, you could always solve a paradox. But only do this if you have to. Goldbach's conjecture, and the Euler-Mascheroni constant are all still available. And there's prize money up for grabs. You are, however, tying yourself to someone else's name tag, and you would do better to find your own idea.

Bodily functions

"Cloning may be good and it may be bad. Probably it's a bit of both. The question must not be greeted with reflex hysteria but decided quietly, soberly and on its own merits. We need less emotion and more thought."
—Richard Dawkins

If you don't fancy physics, biology is hot too. Neuroscience and genetics, in particular. Be the first person to clone yourself. The trouble for the potential genius here is that ethics (welcome back, Socrates!) might become a consideration. But then biology and medicine have always held hands in a bloodstained way—18th-century anatomists were known to resort to grave robbing and even murder if the supply of corpses dried up.

Think about the moral maze if and when you get there. You are propelled forward by the desire to find out. Keep going. Let's be blunt about this genetics thing. Where is it all heading? Eternal life, that's where. That's the public's silent prayer (the public is here understood to mean those in the developed world with money). So, if you and your genetics pals down at the university labs could fix something up, what better way to ensure your name lives forever than by actually living forever?

A skilled hand? Join the arts

Perhaps you like to paint, write, or play the piano? You should consider being an artistic genius. As an artist you see the world in a way that other people don't, until you show them. Then they say, "Oh yes! I see the world like that too. I just didn't realize I did." You make the new familiar and the familiar new. A wicked illusion.

Bear in mind here that it's not necessarily the invention of something that will get you the genius tag. It could be the expertise of its use. Do we remember Filippo Brunelleschi for his work on perspective or do we remember the painters who came after—the da Vincis and Donatellos? Similarly, Shakespeare wasn't too bothered about coming up with his own stories. Thomas Kyd had already written a play called *Hamlet* when Shakespeare decided that, yes, he could probably do something with that gloomy Danish prince story.

Geniuses do homework

If brushes, palettes, and smocks are your thing, consider how history's artistic geniuses have distinguished themselves. Look at all the Renaissance greats: they tended to be apprenticed at an early age to established practitioners, whom they then outshone. Whether you're a painter or a physicist, you have to absorb a lot of stuff before you get to do the business yourself. Even Picasso got plenty of proper painting under his belt before he went all modern. His dad was an art teacher.

Play it again, Wolfgang

"Nor do I hear in my imagination the parts successively,
I hear them all at once. What a delight this is! All this
inventing, this producing, takes place in a pleasing,
lively dream." —Wolfgang Amadeus Mozart

If you like to tinkle the keys, you might want to look to your dad as well. Bach, Mozart, and Beethoven all had heavy-duty dads, driving their progeny on to greatness. If this is currently your situation, bear in mind that your dad, as well as driving you to insanity, should be able to help you get commissions and jobs with the royal family or the pope or at least that soundtrack for the blockbuster movie. Make sure he does his bit. You're his investment too.

Bringin' it all Bach home

Ideally, your music should advance what were previously thought to be the boundaries of the possible in form and/or style. It should also somehow mystically trigger emotional responses in us that make us feel that there are human universals and that they can be felt and you can understand other people and other people can understand you and that all this is somehow significant. Or insignificant if you're in a minor key. Sounds like quite hard work, but composers and musicians are well-known debauchees and slackers, so it probably isn't.

What are words worth?

Writing is just talking written down. Being a genius at it, though, takes a bit of thought and maybe some artful borrowing from other writers. But you do have some choices here. You can always introduce a new form. Who would have thought that nobody had invented the novel until Miguel de Cervantes wrote *Don Quixote?* He saw a gap in the market, filled it with a satirical take on the values of chivalry and medieval romance told as an episodic prose narrative, and now he's wearing his genius badge with appropriate aplomb. And the reading public is saying, "Yes, novels are what we want."

Bard to beat

Another choice is to take complete mastery or "mistressy" of as many forms as possible—tragedy, comedy, history, pastoral, historical-pastoral, tragic-historical, tragic-comical-historical-pastoral—and smash any professional opposition by producing the most unbelievable body of work. Think of Shakespeare's plays. (If you're wondering about the dad thing, Shakespeare's dad was no great shakes. He did get to be mayor of Stratford but he wasn't known for writing sonnets or anything.) What you write must inform and confirm. You need to show people what humanity is and what it can mean and by doing this remind them of their own humanity, of the comedy of love and the tragedy of mortality, and all that sort of stuff. What are you waiting for? Get your notepad.

Got a posse? Try leadership

Can a politician, a monarch, a soldier, or the leader of a Marxist peasant uprising really be classed as a genius? If so, how is their success to be gauged? Lands conquered and enemies slaughtered? The greatest number of live human sacrifices? The longest stretch of peacetime prosperity? The biggest army? The most polished speech?

It seems like an acceptable conversation piece to say that Alexander the Great or Genghis Khan or Erwin Rommel were military geniuses. But it probably isn't. They may have possessed outstanding intellectual ability; they may have bettered all their peers by a country mile, dying with their hands still gripping the levers of power; they may have had intense dads. But Rommel wasn't Newton, and Genghis Khan wasn't Johann Sebastian Bach. It would be a crazy world if they had been.

Alexander vs Aristotle

Let's allow some brain space for the example of Aristotle and Alexander the Great. Alexander went for the option of having power in his lifetime. And for a period of time he must have rightly boasted that he was the mightiest man in the world. Respect! But Aristotle, mere tutor to the boy king, still has his ideas taught today. Obviously, Alexander the Great does get a mention in schools, but as history—a name on the list of great men. Aristotle lives when we think about what he said.

ALEXANDER THE GREAT (356–323 B.C.E.) —WARRIOR KING

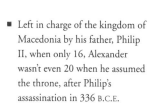

- Left in charge of the kingdom of Macedonia by his father, Philip II, when only 16, Alexander wasn't even 20 when he assumed the throne, after Philip's assassination in 336 B.C.E.

- In his youth, Alexander was tutored by the famous Greek philosopher Aristotle.

- He conquered the Thracians, the Illyrians, the Persian Empire, and much of the then-known world. His years of campaigning took him as far east as India, where he is remembered as "Sikander," a term used as a synonym for "expert."

- In 323 B.C.E., at the age of only 32, but battered and worn after over a decade of fighting, Alexander fell ill following a drinking bout. He died within a fortnight.

- His marriage to Roxana, daughter of Oxyartes of Bactia, was said to be because of her beauty, but it undoubtedly had political advantages as well. The same can be said of his affair with Statira, wife of Darius III—reputed to have been murdered by Roxana.

- Although he is credited with marking the beginning of the Hellenistic Age, Alexander's empire fractured soon after his death as his generals squabbled over the spoils.

Know your field

Once you have decided on a field, you need to know what has been done so that you can know what still needs to be done.

Math and science

These should give you an almost infinite number of ideas.

- Euclid's *Elements*. Want to be big in math? Read this book.
- Newton's *Philosophiae Naturalis Principia Mathematica*. The original manual for the universe.
- Charles Darwin's *The Origin of Species by Means of Natural Selection* is a tome for those interested in origins and species.

Art

Cast your eyes over . . .

- *Adoration of the Magi* by Leonardo da Vinci. Brilliantly unfinished.
- *Birth of Venus* by Sandro Botticelli. You've got to love the flowers.
- *Guernica* by Pablo Picasso. It's a spiky world.

Literature

Obviously the problem of language occurs. So, let's be inclusive.

- Shakespeare is nice and weighty and, of course, contains all you need to know about human nature and its expression in language.

- As a bit of a genius's genius, Johann Goethe really deserves a look. If you speak German, try his *Faust* or *Gotz von Berlichingen.*
- Naturally French needs a look as well. Give anything by Emile Zola or Gustave Flaubert or Alexandre Dumas a read. Formidable!

Music

In one sense music is an international language, in another sense it isn't. Again, inclusivity is a watchword here.

- To wrap your ears around modernity's take on what noises to make in the concert hall, try Schoenberg.
- From Dixieland to Davis, if you like jazz, you'll need to know how to improvise. Go, Cat!
- Listen to the Beatles, the Rolling Stones, Stevie Wonder. Don't listen to anything after 1979.

Philosophy

Chat these around:

- Aristotle produced something called Nichomachean Ethics. It sounds like an espionage novel. But it's so much more.
- When rationalist René Descartes wrote his *Meditations* in 1641, little did he know that "I think therefore I am" was going to provide punning idiots with material for centuries.
- Immanuel Kant's *Critique of Pure Reason* definitely has the killer title here.

Making it your day job

As a genius, you have a reasonable-to-good chance of making some money out of your condition. But some ends are deader than others and you should at least give the money-spinning potential some thought, even if you are "doing it for the benefit of mankind."

If your big idea is something that lots of people are going to want—the lightbulb, say, or the horseless carriage—then you might be up for some serious cash. But if your idea is something like "I think therefore I am," the financial angle is limited.

Philosophers need to sell books and give lectures in order to make money. This is where dumbing it down might help. You need a catchphrase or a theory. Something like "existence precedes essence" or "beyond good and evil."

Musicians, artists, and writers can make a good living. And these days, technology can help you. Beethoven and Mozart gave concerts or got commissions to earn their crusts. They didn't have the advantage of CDs, DVDs, or downloads that they could sell like Britney Spears. Try to like your children, because when you're dead the royalties are theirs.

One final tip: if you're looking to make money as a physicist or a chemist, then nuclear and biological weapons are currently a good earner. You just need the right connections in order to be able to flog the stuff.

CHAPTER FIVE

Maximize Your Potential

"Genius lies not in thinking of ideas, but in the ability to execute the ideas."

JANE McELYEA

MAXIMIZE YOUR POTENTIAL

YOU MIGHT BE THINKING THAT EITHER YOU'RE A GENIUS OR YOU'RE NOT. NICE AND SIMPLE. BUT YOU COULDN'T BE FURTHER FROM THE TRUTH. THERE ARE A NUMBER OF STEPS YOU CAN TAKE TO INCREASE THE LIKELIHOOD OF BLOSSOMING INTO A FIRST-CLASS INTELLECTUAL. BE SURE TO STRIDE THOSE STEPS.

The right kind of surname

As with many aspects of the world of genius, chance has a hand to play even in the story of the actual name that lives forever. Regardless of your brilliant achievement/discovery/invention, a name has to be pretty robust to last forever.

It's probably no accident that the spirit of genius prefers to brush its stardusty fingers against the brows of people with names that stand out. Genius wants memorable. Smith or Jones? Sound like geniuses? Mozart or Michelangelo? You've got to be rare.

TOP FIVE MAGICAL MODIFIERS

- **The Impaler.** This has simplicity, directness, and threat. But you do sound a little like a one-trick pony.

- **The Terrible.** Bluntly put, this one doesn't do it anymore. We live with worldwide terror now. We're too used to it.

- **The Magnificent.** Still good to go, this majestical moniker is general enough to let people's imaginations do the work.

- **The Elder.** It's low-key and classy, it acknowledges your experience and wisdom, but it's probably too understated for the brash 21st century.

- **The Mongoose.** You could go left field and quirky. Though you could also end up sounding like a cartoon character.

Genius jobs

There is a decent range of jobs available to the aspirant intellectual mega-being: from third-rate teacher in a technical college to friend of the most powerful rulers. The tip here is that the top brass, like most of us, are keen on showbiz. So, being the pre-eminent playwright of the Renaissance is going to get you into more of those glossy majesty-and-gleaming-pomp parties than coming up with some linguistic theory about universal grammar.

Year zero

A number of geniuses have started their professional careers in dead-end jobs, only to be rocketed suddenly to the august surroundings of the Royal Society or an echoing papal antechamber. The message here is that if you are currently an unrecognized genius and you're getting a bit worried about how long you've been working as a post-office sorter or bank clerk, stay calm. Fate's finger may yet point you out.

On the other hand, an early start is always good. If you can get a job at an early age working for the king or the emperor or whoever the transient power figure is, all the better. Someone has to pay for all those operas and tragedies; someone has to cover your rent and your groceries while you're thinking the thoughts you need to think. Friends with deep pockets. And it's not really being a parasite—humanity needs you to get on.

A cautionary word about teamwork

Combining genius and teamwork is a dangerous operation. The public wants a single soul to glorify. So we're all supposed to understand that both Crick and Watson figured out the double helix DNA thing? "Well, which one of them figured it out?" asks the head-scratching public, trying to visualize the two of them hunched over a lab bench, test tubes in the background, chatting about complicated stuff, and both realizing something at exactly the same time. The teamwork reputation is never safe. Someone probably did take minutes after all. It's your word against theirs. Much safer to be the lone genius.

Unmanned genius

Darkest history does allow a kind of forgiveness and compromise. Lots of early literature is a collective enterprise, rounded and polished over generations before anyone thought of writing it down. And some of it manages to stand the test of time as great work. Homer's *Iliad* may not all be Homer's *Iliad*, but Homer's *Iliad* it is. *Gilgamesh*? *Beowulf*? Great titles, cultural stepping-stones and all, but who gets the credit? Someone missed an opportunity. The populace will always be uncomfortable with it. It's not the solitary act of heroic greatness that they want. They want a name.

Enter the left-field amateur

A risky but satisfying strategy is to appear suddenly from nowhere. There is a certain aspect of this in genius itself because of its ability to break new ground where no one had previously managed it. The point is that you don't have to be sponsored by an emperor or the church or anything. You can be the genius equivalent of the sleeper cell: making preparations, sharpening your idea, and waiting for your moment.

It is important to stay focused during this period of intellectual exile. Be sure that your colleagues at the institute are all going to comment on how you were "destined for greatness" and "just different from everyone else." Making that sudden lurch for greatness can be a strain, so be certain that you and those around you are ready. But don't make an idiot of yourself. What you have is not the X-factor; it's something else entirely.

Be optimistic

Consider the poet William Blake. He received hardly any recognition during his lifetime. He wasn't taught painting through apprenticeship like your average arty genius; in fact, he was taught by a man who came to him in his dreams. His poetry was seen as crazily idiosyncratic and marginal. It is. And we like that today, even if in 1800 it was seen as nonsense. He deserves credit, though. He remained convinced throughout his life that one day the world would get it. He was right.

ALBERT EINSTEIN (1879–1955)—PHYSICIST

- It took baby Einstein about four years to start talking, and young Einstein could be a difficult and rebellious child.

- Although Einstein was born in Ulm, Germany, he became a Swiss citizen in 1901 and an American citizen in 1940.

- Einstein first published his famous theory of relativity (including the mass–energy equivalence $E=mc^2$) in 1905; however, he had written the ideas in an essay ten years earlier, at the age of 16.

- Einstein's idea that gravitational field should influence the wavelength of light emitted by atoms was proven by observations of a 1919 eclipse.

- In 1939 Einstein signed a letter to President Franklin Roosevelt, written by physicist Leó Szilárd, suggesting that the U.S. government should develop the atom bomb before Germany did. After World War II, however, he lobbied for nuclear disarmament.

- In 1952 he was offered the presidency of Israel. He declined.

Dress the part

"Beauty like hers is genius" —Dante Gabriel Rossetti

There is no single dress code for geniuses. You have to make a judgment about what is appropriate in what context. This, however, is not as simple as it sounds. Even though it is still quite simple.

That tie with *those* shorts?

A toga or a codpiece might be fine in certain circumstances (though you might feel more comfortable collecting your Nobel Prize in the creased and shiny old suit that you bought for your first day of work). It's not always easy for a genius to know what is appropriate, but keeping things straightforward is the key. The lab coat is good for working in the lab, looking down the microscope, doing a double take then looking again, and all that. For expounding your theory to skeptical peers in the university library, a worn-out corduroy sports jacket over unironed shirt, with checked tie and navy V-neck will usually work. Remember to wear trousers and shoes also. For leading the hordes across the steppes in a sweep of mass murder, arson, and pillage, plenty of animal-hide combinations and a few trinkets made from the skulls and teeth of your vanquished foes. All these suggestions are simple but appropriate.

Act the part

Whether you're an attic-dwelling artistic genius, or a dungeon-dwelling mathematical genius, you will need to act the part. People expect it. And besides, it's being yourself.

If you are the artistic-genius-type, your role is to investigate the human condition. This may involve debauched and "alternative" sexual behaviors, huge gambling debts, syphilis, mental health problems, and an early grave. It appeals to a romantic notion we have about creativity and social skills.

Do not disturb

At the other end of the spectrum you may need to be aloof, above the merely human. Your genius thinking might be about math or physics, in which case your behavior should eschew human relationships and their messy illogicality. Smudgy human relationships are a distraction from the stratospheric realm of pure numerical relationships.

If you must have human contact and friendship, find someone with whom you can talk equations. You should be able to locate at least one other person who cares what x is. Better to spend most of your time in front of a blackboard, chalk in hand, stacking up those big numbers and letters that stand for numbers in ever-more-complex combinations. A good sum is like a neat refrain from a Bach cantata—detailed, beautiful, and rigorous. It's your instrument—play that thing!

REHEARSE SOME LINES

Here are a few things that might be uttered by a genius. Try them on for size.

- "You're overlooking one small but essential fact, professor."
- "Parmenion will advance the troops at my command!"
- "Cappuccino to go, please, Raoul."
- "I'm like, 'Put the poker down, dude.'"
- "Thomas, when you advance, draw your sword straightaway. Think motivation. You're going to murder the king, darling."
- "And the process gives off a gas. A vapor of startling odor, which, when inhaled, brings forth feelings of extraordinary peculiarity. Try it."
- "This creature could destroy me. My work!"

Or . . .

- "Eureka!"
- "I think therefore I am."
- "You're a monkey."
- "Mistakes are the portals of discovery."
- "I refute it thus!"
- "Thank you, madam, the agony is abated."
- "It is not enough to succeed. Others must fail."

You will have noticed that some of the rehearsal statements end with punctuation signaling exclamation. Don't doubt it—part of the attraction of being a genius is the excitement. Just ask Archimedes. He got so excited by his groundbreaking idea that he ran naked through the streets.

CHAPTER SIX

Genius at Large

—— ◆ ——

"Genius . . . means the transcendent
capacity of taking trouble."

THOMAS CARLYLE

GENIUS AT LARGE

BELIEVE IT OR NOT, PEOPLE SOMETIMES DON'T WANT TO HEAR WHAT A GENIUS HAS TO SAY. YOU SHOULD BEAR THIS IN MIND IF YOUR PARTICULAR GENIUS INVOLVES DELIVERING, ON BEHALF OF ALL OF HUMANITY, SOME UNCOMFORTABLE TRUTHS.

Muzzled

Sometimes it's not that they won't listen; it's that they are not allowed to listen. Take Galileo, for instance. He dared to publish a comparison of the Ptolemaic and Copernican systems and concluded, convincingly, that Copernicus was right—everything revolves around the sun. This was not a view popular with the church, and Galileo's judgment that he would probably get away with it turned out to be of the non-genius order. He was under house arrest for the rest of his days.

You can prove it

One reason the church was so uncomfortable with Galileo was that he stepped into a conceptual no-go zone. Galileo, a highly respected and accomplished man, crossed the line and said, "No. It is not theory; it is *true*. The earth is not the center of the universe. The math proves it." That's what the church didn't like. The "it's true" bit and the "math proves it" bit.

Badge of honor

From the middle of the 16th century, the Catholic church published a list of works that printers were not allowed to produce. Perhaps slightly embarrassing for Popes Paul IV, Pius IV, Leo XIII, and so on, is that a good number of the books on the *Index Librorum Prohibitorum* are now seen as landmarks in the history of intellectual development.

The Index

Yes, the *Index Librorum Prohibitorum*. The books the Vatican thought you shouldn't read. It's a veritable Who's Who of brain power, the cream of the crop. Banned and proud.

1. **Nicolaus Copernicus.** Why would he be banned? He dedicated *De Revolutionibus Orbium Coelestium* to the Pope. Did they think he was being ironic?

2. **René Descartes.** *Thinking about God* is a tricky one. In one way the church does want you to think about God. But to think about God in other ways is not to be encouraged.

3. **Desiderius Erasmus.** Poor old Erasmus, surely not banned for the seemingly harmless title *The Praise of Folly*.

4. **Galileo Galilei.** The earth goes round the sun? Ban him!

5. **Immanual Kant.** Banned for the *Critique of Pure Reason*. Enough with the critiquing of pure reason, already.

6. **Niccolò Machiavelli.** His name is enough to give you the creeps.

7. **John Stuart Mill.** What Mill is doing is taking ideas about liberty and morality away from the church. He is on their turf and they are not going to stand for it.

Some people just don't like a brainiac

A current problem in our schools is the idea that learning is not "cool." This is, in a sense, a big idea. Its effect is certainly big. But it is not a genius idea. It is a doofus idea. It is evidence of a point of view that has dogged the advancement of mankind and the development of individual genius.

Many societies have (probably) shown a broad streak of anti-intellectualism whereby the intellectual is feared because of his or her superior knowledge. He or she might be able to prove that your understanding of the forces that shape your existence is limited. No one likes that. And sometimes, if people don't like you, they do something about it.

Some people simply hate a brainiac

Hypatia of Alexandria, charismatic teacher of mathematics and philosophy, was probably murdered by Christians who felt threatened by her Neoplatonist views. Socrates also managed to annoy too many people with his cheeky questioning and his philosophizing. Death by hemlock for him.

The ability to die by being murdered is particularly noteworthy in the case of the political or leadership genius. Especially if, like the probably poisoned Ivan the Terrible, you have made enemies aplenty through a personal policy of orgiastic excess and a public policy of mass murder. But then he's not such a good example. He wasn't a genius. He was a nut.

HYPATIA OF ALEXANDRIA (370–415 C.E.)
—PHILOSOPHER

- Employed in the Temple of the Muses at the Great Library of Alexandria, Hypatia's father was Theon, an astronomer, mathematician, and teacher. He taught his daughter.

- Victorians Charles Kingsley and Charles William Mitchell were fascinated by Hypatia. Kingsley wrote a novel based on her life and she was the inspiration for Mitchell's most notable painting.

- She lectured on Platonist philosophy in Alexandria and Athens and attracted students from all over the Greek world.

- In her role as a teacher, Hypatia once had to deter a student who had fallen in love with her by throwing sanitary towels repeatedly at him.

- There exist different theories about her death, but Hypatia seems to have been murdered by a mob that was determined to silence such an influential pagan in what was becoming an increasingly Christian culture.

- One historian, Bishop John of Nikiu, perhaps wanting to ingratiate himself with Cyril, Bishop of Alexandria at the time of Hypatia's death, portrays her as a witch, beguiling men and leading them away from the church.

The late-in-life genius

The idea that you can discover your hidden genius in your twilight years is a bit of a myth. It is possible that after a lifetime of dedicated work as a moderately successful civil servant you might retire and think about writing the novel that you always felt was in you but you just never had time for, what with the job, the family, and the mortgage. You might write that novel and craft it over the next five years, so that when you send it to a publisher and you become a worldwide publishing sensation, you are already in your 70s. You are then lauded by the literary elite as that rare thing—the as-yet-undiscovered genius. So to die of a heart attack at the age of 68, only days before an interview for a big feature in the *New York Times*, seems a bit sad. It is sad. Avoid it.

The outsider

- Tormented by mental illness
- Ground down by poverty, lack of success, and stubbornness
- Driven to cut off part of his own ear and give it to a prostitute
- Thirty-seven years old when he shot himself in the chest in a field

It can only be Vincent van Gogh. On the very verge of going big, the manic redhead decided he couldn't take it. Sometimes the genius life is sad and short.

Getting recognized and avoiding execution at all costs

If, by this time, you've realized you are a source of dazzling, world-shaking ideas, you will need to get those ideas disseminated. Your primary aim at this point is to get publicity. Once your genius is recognized, you will have a serious profile. You may well make enemies. Here are ten tips for achieving your primary aim at this point—staying alive:

- Get to know an emperor or a pope or a Florentine prince. You need sponsorship to get your stuff out there.

- Persevere.

- Don't cross the Athenian people or the Christian church.

- Have some sophistry ready, in case the authorities come for you.

- Persevere.

- If you absolutely must court controversy, make sure to keep it inside the department.

- Get your dad involved.

- Be sure that you're not just nuts rather than a proper genius.

- In general, keep your eccentricities unthreatening.

- Persevere.

CHAPTER SEVEN

The Evil Genius

———◆———

"The belief in a supernatural source of evil is
not necessary; men alone are quite capable
of every wickedness."

JOSEPH CONRAD

THE EVIL GENIUS

EVIL IS REALLY NOT SOMETHING THAT SHOULD BE ENCOURAGED. IF YOU ARE AN INTELLECTUAL SUPER-BEING YOU SHOULD BE THINKING ABOUT HOW TO PUT YOUR BRILLIANCE TO USE FOR THE GOOD OF HUMANITY. BUT IF YOU'RE NASTY AND YOU KNOW IT, READ ON.

A question of morality

Ambition doesn't require a basis in morality—just ask Macbeth. Machiavelli will tell you that having morals can positively be a hindrance. Certainly, in terms of leadership, a lack of moral scruples can be a real bonus.

Foster your ruthlessness streak

Leadership is where evil genius really comes into its own. That's because leadership is about manipulating people, not numbers, shapes, or chemicals. People are affected by morality in ways that numbers, shapes, and chemicals are not. An equilateral triangle has no moral resonance (unless it's a love triangle, but even then it's a metaphor). Similarly, it's hard to see a trapezoid as evil or Mendeleyev's table of elements as morally bankrupt and wicked.

If you are all about power, people will be prepared to fight you for that power, and you will have to be prepared to fight back. But then again, the cut and thrust isn't limited solely to the worlds of political and military might. You might have enemies in the chemistry department. There might be people who want to see your professional career fail. A touch of ruthlessness of character never went amiss for even the best of the good-hearted geniuses.

NICCOLÒ MACHIAVELLI (1469–1527)—POLITICAL PHILOSOPHER, MUSICIAN, POET, PLAYWRIGHT

- Only very few geniuses get to have their names turned into an adjective—"Machiavellian" means cunning, opportunistic, and deceitful. For a Machiavellian character, the ends justify the means.

- *Il Principe* (*The Prince*) is Machiavelli's most famous work. It is an analysis of the manipulation of political power and marks a shift from the idealism of Plato to a new Renaissance realism.

- As a Florentine diplomat for over a decade, Machiavelli was well placed to study the turbulent political atmosphere of his day and to meet its major figures. He was particularly inspired by Cesare Borgia.

- In his text *Discorsi* (*Discourses*), Machiavelli sets out a series of lessons on how a republic should be established, structured, and governed. His brilliant political philosophy underpins many democracies today.

- In 1513 he was tortured on the rack for his alleged role in a political plot, but maintained his innocence. He was pardoned but exiled, where he continued writing his treatises.

- As a true Renaissance man, Machiavelli also wrote plays. His racy satirical comedy *La Mandragola* (*The Mandrake*) was a hit.

The monster's tale

Genius—particularly scientific genius—is haunted by the specter of "Frankenstein's monster." Frankenstein's monster represents the unforeseen effect, the arrogant genius losing possession of his or her ever-more-uncontrollable creation.

For example, the ability to split the atom soon led to military ramifications. Marie Curie was, in a tragedy of the Aristotelian sense, laid low by her own achievement—though not through hubris. Despite being the first woman to receive a Nobel Prize, her death was most probably caused by exposure to the radioactive materials she discovered. The irony is that Curie was caught in the Frankenstein narrative even though she was not an evil genius. So be warned that your good genius work could morph into evil genius material. You might start off wondering if an atom can be split and end up showing a general what happens when you do.

Frankenstein's Monster Sydrome

- Avoid selling your soul in exchange for instant fame
- Don't buy a medieval castle in the Carpathians
- Stop the experiment if you start to feel guilt mixing with the arrogance
- Ask yourself if it really is for the good of mankind
- Try not to focus solely on "the power to create life itself!"

Can tyrants be geniuses?

"My presence scares happiness away; and good deeds
grow powerless, when I become concerned in them.
Fugitive, unresting I should be, that my evil genius might
not seize me . . . " —J. W. Goethe

The question is whether wickedly evil tyrants can display genius characteristics. And the answer has to be yes, though they're few and far between. The thing about the evil tyrant-style genius, if you're considering such a career path, is that it's really difficult to make your mark in an immortal, genius kind of way. There are, observably, different levels of tyranny, and you stand out by being the most murderous or the cruellest killer. But is this genius? Someone like Robert Mugabe is a fairly successful tyrant, but quite obviously not a genius. The question, or one question, is whether the exercise of an outstanding intellect can be seen in the actions of a wicked despot.

Was Stalin a genius? Was Hitler a genius? Our judgment here is all about power management and strategic acumen. Were Hitler and Stalin demonstrating outstanding intellect when they turned their enemies against each other and consolidated their control? No. They were just clever bullies writ large. It probably wasn't an act of genius to purge the Soviet army's officers on the eve of German invasion. It probably wasn't an act of genius to delay the southerly movement of the panzers because the Normandy landings appeared to be a feint. (Although we should keep in mind that having stupid ideas doesn't necessarily disqualify you from genius status. Newton, of all people, was convinced that alchemy was a viable pursuit.) The big two despots of the 20th century were ruthless, evil, and had bucketloads of cunning. But that didn't make them geniuses.

Isn't it good to be feared?

Admiration and awe are what you're really going for when you sign up for genius status. They are often enjoyable consequences of genius and occasionally form strong workable motivational tools as you work late into the night on your genius concepts.

But fear is a different thing. Fear as an end in itself or as a means of controlling people's lives somehow doesn't quite sit with being a genius. Fear is the means by which tyrants stop their subjects thinking or talking about new ideas. But geniuses like new ideas. If a tyrant does like a new idea it is probably a new idea about how to kill enemies, destroy their citadels, and lay waste their lands. This is all right, but can be a bit of a bore. From the bow and arrow to the laser-guided bomb, it's all about killing people. So don't throw your life's work into ways of exterminating others if only because it's been done so much before. It's not exactly akin to a revelation like "species adapt to their environments through a process of evolution" or "for a right-angle triangle with legs a and b and hypotenuse c, $a^2 + b^2 = c^2$." Is it?

One of us

The ideal combination, if despotism and tyranny are your thing, is to be admired by your people and feared by your enemies. Where your enemies regard you as aggressive and brutal, your people must see you as strong and confident. Following are some thinking points for the aspiring evil genius.

Retain your reason

Despite the fact that you are insanely evil, you still need reason. Consider Stalin's use of equation: death solves all problems; therefore, no man = no problem. Very simple, very "big picture," very cause and effect. Totally evil too, of course.

Become a cult figure

Once you achieve power you should get yourself mythologized. This often happens to geniuses once they are dead, but you need to get it happening sooner. Achieve this by setting up a ministry of propaganda, inventing proverbial episodes from your childhood, and ensuring that every sculpture is of you.

Your attitude toward violence

You will either need to feel ambivalent toward violence or to actually like it. When Napoleon said that the carnage at

Borodino was "the most beautiful battlefield I've ever seen," he meant it.

You're the team captain

As a ruthless leader, you will need the help of others—flunkies, sycophants, yes-men. You will at times have to delegate power. Your genius is for managing those who exercise power on your behalf, creating structures of political machinery that allow you control. Go, Captain!

You're history

> "The man of genius . . . is an originator, an inspired or demonic man, who produces a perfect work in obedience to laws yet unexplored." —Henry David Thoreau

The evil genius is probably not remembered for a series of world-changing ideas. It's no accident that Plato's philosopher kings are ideal rather than real rulers. The evil genius is remembered as one of history's do-ers rather than as one of science or philosophy's thinkers.

You might be remembered by some colorful sobriquet. Who wouldn't want to be remembered as, say, Jeremy "the Impaler" or Peaches "the Merciless"? But these adjectival accessories really only serve to point out that you were Terrible or Great, not that you thought anything new. King Richard gets remembered for his Lionheart rather than his Godbrain. Even the mysterious "Genghis Khan" only means Genghis the Chief.

CHAPTER EIGHT

Genius and Romance

———◆———

"Beware you are not swallowed up in books!
An ounce of love is worth a pound
of knowledge."

JOHN WESLEY

GENIUS AND ROMANCE

OBVIOUSLY, THE QUESTION ON EVERYONE'S LIPS IS HOW BEING A GENIUS AFFECTS YOUR LOVE LIFE. IS BEING A BRAINIAC GOING TO GET YOU THE GIRL OR GUY? OF COURSE, EROS, *AMOUR*—WHATEVER YOU WANT TO CALL IT— WILL ALSO ENSURE THAT THERE ARE TIMES WHEN THE HEART RULES THE HEAD. YOU MIGHT THINK THAT'S BAD FOR SOMEONE WHO IS ALL ABOUT BRAIN POWER. YOU MIGHT BE RIGHT.

The IQ aphrodisiac

Dinner with a mad-professor type? What comes to mind? An absence of romantic mood, lashings of social ineptitude, a funny voice prattling on about quasars and dark matter?

Consider the Jerry Lewis film *The Nutty Professor*. The alchemic "potion" the professor drinks turns him from the geekishly nerdy Professor Julius Kelp into the slick and sensual Buddy Love. The lothario and the intellectual are presented as opposites. But the film's message, thankfully for us all, is that it doesn't have to be that way. Intellectuals are attractive for what they are. Knowledge is power. Power is attractive.

The few successful ones

Blanket assertions aside (or in theoretical parentheses), there may be problems balancing intellectual activity and *la vie d'amour*. It really does depend on your chosen field.

Shakespeare got to hang out with aristocrats and the theater crowd. (It should be remembered that there were no actresses in 1600, so theater was yet to become the hotbed of dressing-room shenanigans that it is today). Dickens liked to get out and meet his adoring fans through public readings. His mistress was an actress. Picasso set the standard though—a ballerina, an artist, a photographer—all sorts of complicated offspring stuff. So focusing on the performing or visual arts seems a good bet if your intellectual curiosity has a smoochy side.

Love in the lab

The lab is a place of work and as such as good a place as any to meet a spouse. But be realistic. The prospective bedmate you meet in a lab is unlikely to be a countess or a love-crazed bohemian. More likely an assistant or a cleaner.

As a literary genius, you might pen a number of love sonnets, which will be gold dust in any long-distance epistolary seduction. As an artistic genius, you may paint a portrait of the object of your desire that leaves no doubt as to the depth and authenticity of your love. However, collecting your own urine, letting it putrefy, and then heating it to condense its vapors all in the name of scientific investigation is less adaptable in terms of using the product of your intellect to attract mates.

The problem of remembering your spouse's name

If you were Picasso, you could be forgiven for forgetting your spouse's name. For heaven's sake, he married so many. However, for most geniuses the problem is more to do with having your mind over-crammed with difficult stuff. It's easy for something as mundane as the name of your spouse or firstborn to disappear under a mountain of far-more-important detail. It is therefore advisable for prospective geniuses to carry an index card listing useful names and addresses—including their own.

WILLIAM SHAKESPEARE (1564–1616)
—PLAYWRIGHT, POET, ACTOR

- Born the son of a glover and civic official, William had two brothers and four sisters.

- At the age of 19, he married Anne Hathaway, who was 26 years old and pregnant.

- Legend has it that he ran away to London because he was caught poaching. But Shakespeare was not a bad businessman and it might be more likely that he went to London to make money.

- As well as writing about 38 plays and more than 150 sonnets and other poems, Shakespeare acted too, and is known to have performed for Queen Elizabeth I.

- Speculation continues as to whether William Shakespeare from Stratford did indeed write all of the works attributed to him. Candidates for alternative authorship include the playwright Christopher Marlowe; Edward de Vere, Earl of Oxford; and philosopher and statesman Sir Francis Bacon.

- Just as Shakespeare was building a reputation as a playwright, London theaters were closed down because of the plague in 1593. Shakespeare stayed in the capital but switched to poetry for a while.

The Mrs. Einstein syndrome

Just as in domestic life, it might be that, professionally your partner is your competitor. This could be a problem. Why? Well, do you want to share your Nobel Prize?

Consider the case of the man who came to exemplify genius in the 20th century. A series of groundbreaking and physics-reshaping publications established Einstein as the big boss of understanding the universe. Or did it? Might he have been assisted by someone whom history did not choose to deify? Might that person have been his first wife, Mileva Marič? Possibly, but probably not. She was a brainy, scientific type and she may have helped Albert out, but the evidence that they collaborated in-depth is scant.

And since you're wondering, the case for an Einstein conspiracy is flimsy. It is known that he discussed ideas with two other physics fans, Conrad Habicht and Maurice Solovine (quite good genius names, but not top-notch). The three men formed a little discussion group they called the Olympia Academy. But it seems they discussed . . . philosophy.

What the comfy slippers of cultural remembering wants is the story of the puppet and the puppet mistress. A conspiracy version. But unfortunately this isn't the case. The moral of the story goes something like: "marry a moron." That way, the historians and hagiographers can be sure it was all your own work and there will be no tarnish on your shiny reputation.

Unlucky in love

In case this genius caper isn't working out for you, there's some consolation to be felt in the fact that many geniuses are notoriously unlucky in love. Nineteenth-century philosophy buff Friedrich Nietzsche might have been a brilliant thinker but he was on the Loserville Express when it came to the ladies.

Nietzsche may have suffered repeated rejection because he was a gloomy and manic kind of guy. He was also probably done in by syphilis, possibly contracted from a prostitute that he claims he was forced to sleep with when university pals kidnapped him and took him to the best little whorehouse in Saxony. Those crazy intellectuals!

The genius of love

However, it's just possible that you might be thinking that love itself is your field of expertise. This is what Giovanni Giacomo Casanova thought. In his time he worked for the church and the army and was a diplomat, spy, writer, businessman, and amateur philosopher. But passion was his real passion, and he's remembered as being the genius of love in a way that rock 'n' rollers, actors, and other artistes are not. This is because, for him, seduction and sex were not perks of the trade, they *were* the trade. In his autobiography he claims to have slept with more than 120 women. He has the right kind of name to be a genius, but what was his big idea? "Sleeping with lots of people is good"? Hardly seems original.

Seduction tips

Should you desire to seduce another genius, consider the following approaches:

- When you meet a fellow mega-mind say things like, "Your ideas make me . . . hot" or "IQ scores are so erotic."

- Wear low-cut lab coats.

- Hang out in galleries, fainting occasionally.

- Hang out at the Patent Office, fainting occasionally.

- Hang out at the CERN Accelerator Complex, fainting for an incomprehensibly brief period of time.

Love and the punishing schedule

While aspiring to Casanova heights of romance, remember that sometimes a punishing love schedule can interfere with the punishing schedule of being a genius.

In the case of the Marquis de Sade, philosopher and pornographer (a rare but impressive combination), the big idea was that nature shows no morality and thus morality is unnatural. (If he was so keen on being "natural," one wonders why he bothered living in a house or wearing clothes). He thus pursued a life of amoral sexual pleasure, which gained him an enviable notoriety. But while Nietzsche—a dismal failure in the game of love—is remembered for his brain stuff, de Sade—bedding bevies of babes daily—is not remembered for the lifechanging ideas he bequeathed to us, but just for really walking the walk. His most famous book has two titles: *One Hundred Days of Sodom* or *The School of Freedoms*. By which do you think it is remembered?

The point is that if you are a thinker and a mad sexual libertine at the same time, the public, being the ravenous scandal puppies they are, may overlook your ideas. This is not what you want. If you are an amoral sex machine, keep it out of the papers.

How to be both a lover and a thinker

The next time you are at an intimate soiree, you might like to try out some of the following lines. Not all of them will be appropriate. Context will help you judge.

- "Yes, my dear, but I was thinking of a different kind of chemistry."

- "I can paint you as you'd like to see yourself."

- "My mind may be with the wind-blown clouds, but other parts of me are closer to earth."

- "Come to my garret and I'll show you the stars."

- "If you'll meet me at my lab, I need someone to hold my Bunsen burner."

- "You are the aria in my opera, the sonata in my symphony. Let me call you 'No. 45.'"

- "I'm working on an alternative political philosophy for establishing a republic in this time of social upheaval and global turmoil. But I sometimes take breaks. Got time for a cappuccino?"

- "I speak 18 languages. I can't say 'no' in any of them."

- "I'll take over a country for you, my love. Take your pick."

- "Eureka, baby!"

CHAPTER NINE

On Being Remembered

"Here lies one whose name was
written in water."

JOHN KEATS'S EPITAPH

ON BEING REMEMBERED

THERE'S LITTLE POINT IN BEING A GENIUS IF YOU DON'T GET YOUR PAGE IN THE GREAT BOOK OF HUMAN PROGRESS. DON'T BE LIKE KEATS. GET YOURSELF SOME REPUTATION.

Overnight enlightenment

It is long past midnight. The night is cold and the wind whips the attic roof and rattles the loose skylight. On the little writing table, the candle gutters, its yellow light dancing on the green glass of an empty wine bottle. You are hunched over your parchment, coughing and wheezing and sniffing and trying to finish a sonnet about the physical manifestation of passion in first love. At the back of your mind quotidian worries push against your poetic imagination. You have no money for food or rent and don't know where you will get it. You have coughed up blood again today. Another of the many voices in your head indignantly repeats what it always says: "This isn't right. You are a genius."

And then . . .

The following week, the earl of Daventry is sending a carriage to collect you from your hotel. You have spent the afternoon in your suite being soft-soaped, shaved, and rubbed down by a most comely young woman provided by the maitre d'hotel, and the earl's physician has made a brief visit, during which he counseled you to put worry aside—for the prognosis is good—and has made an appointment for some blood-letting next week. The earl's carriage takes you to the townhouse salon of Countess Daphne of Huntingdon, where you are to give a private reading from your new and extensive collection of mock-classical lyrics.

Once at the salon, and having read your work to warm appreciation and applause, you are introduced to a number of most attractive actresses, poets from Paris, painters from Prague, and playwrights from Philadelphia. Each declares you to be in possession of a rare kind of genius. You have a series of fascinating conversations, drinking the countess's delightful sherry and smoking some fine tobacco newly shipped from Virginia. It is a thoroughly pleasurable evening.

The denouement

But now the smoke is too much and breathing becomes difficult. Why is everyone laughing and drinking and smiling when you can hardly breathe? The reason is that you are not at the townhouse salon. You are still in your garret and you have lapsed into unconsciousness. You cannot breathe because the candle has set fire to the sheaf of poems on the table and now the table itself, and the filthy, ragged curtains are burning fiercely, filling your domicile with dense fumes. You half-manage to wake yourself. The smoke and flames are now so thick and fierce that it is difficult to find your bearings. It occurs to you that you may die. Yes, being catapulted to fame is only a dream.

Wake up to the dream

"Never expect any recognition here—the system prohibits it. The cross is not affixed to the genius, no, the genius is affixed to the cross." —Franz Grillparzer

It's a dream that has 21st-century western culture in its thrall. And it's easy to buy into. You just need to be on television in order for people to think you're some kind of genius. But being on television probably means you're not a genius. While genius often means fame, fame rarely means genius. Cultural achievement, even if you're Mozart, takes a while and some practice to get going. If you're not out and about getting your reputation going, you run the risk of posthumous recognition without a scrap of contemporary adoration, or "doing a Franz Kafka," as it's known.

This problem, however, is less evident in the sciences. If you happen to invent the pasteurization process or publish a full table of elements then you get the job done in one go and you can sit back and sharpen your pencil. Like all sorts of stuff, it's about choice.

Slow-burning reputation and the waves of history

> "If you are a genius and unsuccessful, everybody treats
> you as if you were a genius, but when you come to be
> successful . . . everybody no longer treats you like a
> genius, [but] like a man who has become successful."
> —Pablo Picasso

Reputation, once bid farewell, is never seen again. So they say. But it's not true. Reputation can burn slowly for a time before it catches; it can be a rising and falling wave; it can be represented by any number of metaphors. You can almost disappear from the map of human knowledge, understanding, and creativity and still come charging back to greatness and glory. Your revelatory idea might fade, superseded by better, neater ideas, or it may become increasingly important as the decades and centuries roll by.

The test of time

Think of Charles Darwin and Karl Marx. Both massive names who earned their own adjectives. Their ideas infuse our thinking about ourselves, our societies, our relationships, our very humanity. You can't ask much more from a genius than that. But how have their reputations changed since those heady early days?

Darwin, with elegant understatement, uses the word "evolve" only once in *Origin of Species*. It's the last word in the book. And threatening to be a last word, it's an idea that still draws people into heated arguments and acts of bizarre legislation today. The world's great religions know that it means them no good. Darwin knew it. We all know it.

Marx's ideas changed the lives of many more millions of people than Darwin in much more practical ways. And his ideas are still doing the rounds. You don't have to look too far into the third world to find a Marxist guerrilla movement or uprising. But Marx has lost ground. As a critical framework for historians, social scientists, and the like, Marxism is still a useful tool. As an ideological position in an actively political sense, it's got a dated feel.

So two genius hotshots have their big ideas interpreted in very different ways in very different eras. Beware the revisionist tendencies of those who come after you. Try to be cleverer than they are in order to be sure you come out on top.

Tomorrow and tomorrow . . .

Who knows what is to come? Who knows who we will be in centuries ahead? Perhaps ideas being thought at this very moment, this actual second—your ideas—will influence the lives of millions of future inhabitants of the earth. One thing we do know is that genius ideas never stop coming. Or they haven't so far.

Will the future leave you behind altogether and for good?

There's no doubt about it. Whether or not a genius is remembered, or indeed how that genius is remembered, changes according to contemporary fashion. This is most apparent in the arts, but can be apparent in the sciences too.

We are currently surrounded by "genetic this" and "genome that," so the DNA double-helix guys, Crick and Watson, still have serious reputation. And Darwin sits at the back of all this with an adoring chimp on his knee.

We also like physics, the mind-bending complexity of it and its promise to solve the big questions about the universe. Stephen Hawking is popular, not so much for what he says as for fitting in with our popular mythologies by being a futuristic half-machine-half-super-brain, the robotic voice of the atom age. Behind this sits Einstein, atop Newton's shoulders.

Avoid being a Faraday

We are a bit bored with other aspects of science, however. Just ask Michael Faraday. If you are fanatical about electricity then Faraday is your man. Very big in his day. Or Nikola Tesla, perhaps, whose ideas came to him in flashes of blinding light. Their problem is that you are probably not fanatical about electricity. Electricity has changed our lives, but does it change the way we think about our lives? The egghead of the

21st century doesn't want to make up electrical circuits in the back bedroom. That egghead is more likely to be writing some computer code and thinking that Bill Gates is a genius because he's the richest man in the universe and lives on his own moon.

Faraday's message to the young geniuses of today is that the future may take all your ideas and forget about you, or decide that your epiphanies are just not needed anymore.

Remembered, but not for the reasons you thought

Perhaps you expect to be remembered for your operas rather than your symphonies, or evermore lauded by literate lovers for your verse epics rather than your sonnets. It might not be so much of a surprise to you to find that the opposite occurs. Oh well, tastes change. You could probably get used to it.

But imagine yourself as a philosopher whose only desire is to be loved and published so you can get your ideas out there for other big brains to discuss over an espresso or two. Try hard. Keep imagining, so you can imagine how it would feel to look down from your cloud, only half a century after you shuffled off the coil, to see one of modern history's top crazy dictators using you and your name as supposed inspiration for more mad stuff. And you'd thought living with syphilis was bad enough.

MARIE SKLODOWSKA-CURIE (1867–1934) —PHYSICIST, CHEMIST

- Born in Warsaw, in then Russian-occupied Poland, Marie Sklodowska studied secretly at what was known as the "Flying University" before going to Paris to study physics and mathematics at the Sorbonne.

- Marie married her tutor, Pierre Curie, and together they carried out pioneering work on radioactivity. They were the first to isolate the elements radium and polonium.

- The 1903 Nobel Prize for physics was awarded jointly to Marie, Pierre, and Henri Becquerel for their work with radium. In 1911 Curie became the first person to be awarded Nobel Prizes in two fields, when she was awarded the prize for chemistry.

- After her husband was killed in a motor accident in Paris, Curie scandalized many by having an affair with one of her married colleagues.

- The element Curium is named after Marie and Pierre, as is the unit of radiation, the Curie.

- Her death was almost certainly brought about by long-term exposure to radiation. Her notes and papers are still radioactive and are stored in special containers.

CHAPTER TEN

The Legacy of Genius

"No legacy is so rich as honesty."

WILLIAM SHAKESPEARE

THE LEGACY OF GENIUS

VERY RICH FROM THE BARD, WHOSE ONLY LEGACY TO HIS WIFE WAS HIS
SECOND-BEST BED! ANYWAY, NOW THAT YOU'RE SURE YOU'RE ON THE ROAD
TO BEING A TOP-FLIGHT GENIUS, YOU NEED TO THINK ABOUT WHAT KIND OF
HISTORICAL AND CULTURAL FOOTPRINT YOU'RE GOING TO LEAVE BEHIND.
LET'S HOPE IT'S HUMAN.

Being a cultural icon

Have you got the look? Has your look ever been recorded? A variety of media will work—marble bust, oil on canvas, photograph, clay. You know what people are like: they like to be able to put a face to the name. If you're very lucky, your face can become iconic. Think Einstein, think Shakespeare, think Marx.

If your face is memorable, you're memorable. Think what you can do with your facial hair to make yourself stand out or look intellectual. You might even be able to achieve icon status without using your own face. In an odd way, Michelangelo's statue *David* is Michelangelo. In an even odder way, the *Mona Lisa* is da Vinci.

Becoming iconic means that you end up representing more than just yourself or your ideas. You come to epitomize something about genius itself.

Cuddly Uncle Albert

Albert Einstein, today at least, epitomizes the very center of the kernel of the essence of genius. His ideas were radical, counterintuitive, and very complicated. Yet his image—most importantly the image of him as an old man—helps us not to feel intimidated by his greatness. He looks a bit unkempt, like a kindly grandparent, and he was famously photographed poking his tongue out, so he also has a nice, informal thing going on.

Modeling your look on Einstein's might seem like a sensible strategy, but it is difficult to pull off effectively—particularly if you are a woman. In addition, trying to look like Albert the Brainy will smack of imitation and lack of originality. These are not genius traits.

Will power

Shakespeare manages to epitomize a particularly important time in English history as well as English literature. An intellectual, cultural, and imperial explosion is beginning. Shakespeare puts it all in his plays. But his picture, in particular the Chandos portrait, also manages to represent the idea of the genius writer—observant, aloof, inscrutable.

The workers' beard

Marx is all about the beard. The beard itself, in a general sense rather than just Marx's, has long been a signifier of wisdom and experience. Marx uses it well. His full, impressive growth and gray halo make his head look big and thus full of knowledge and learning. The beard and the eyebrows shout their disregard for appearance ("appearance isn't truth, you fool!") and hint at long nights in the study leafing through many a weighty tome. The iconic image of Marx encapsulates the years of reading and thought a genius puts in—the head-cramming stuff.

"Oh, the razor guy!"

The other thing you can do is get yourself a memorable gimmick that is inseparable from your name. Occam's razor is memorable and arouses our curiosity. What did a mathematician want with a razor? Archimedes's principle is kind of memorable ("the buoyant force is equal to the weight of the displaced fluid"—catchy or what?) and Archimedes's screw sort of stays in the mind. But what we really all remember is Archimedes jumping out of his bath, the public nudity, and shouting, "Eureka!" So get yourself a tagline, a catchphrase, or at the very least, a memorable accessory to attach to your big idea.

GENIUS GIMMICKS

Want to stand out from the genius crowd? Get yourself a gimmick.

- **Albert Einstein.** Einstein's gimmick was a rejection of the stuffy formality of academe. He chose to lecture in scruffy sweaters and carpet slippers.

- **Arthur Schopenhauer.** It is extreme, but Schopenhauer resorted to pushing old ladies down stairs. It's certainly quirky.

- **Diogenes.** Diogenes of Sinope deserves recognition for deciding that the way to distinguish himself from all those heavyweight Greek philosophers was to live in a barrel.

Why we need to believe in genius

If genius didn't exist we'd have to invent it. And perhaps we did. We certainly invented the word.

A bit of philology at this juncture might not do any harm. (Philology might seem like a big word, but it isn't really. It only has nine letters—the same as "mushrooms." Can't be that hard. Etymology if you prefer. Same number of letters. What is important is where the word came from.) "Genius" is Latin (possibly related to *genie*, the Frenchified version of the Arabic *jinni* too) and it means "guardian spirit of a person or place."

So the term "genius" already comes with a built-in godlike, superpower angle. But it only starts to mean what we want it to mean in the 17th century. The Enlightenment needed plenty of geniuses to cast off the gloomy intellectual cobwebs of the Dark Ages, so that's why this word turned up—to describe them.

Anything's possible

Suppose, however, that there is no such thing as genius. That there are only millions of people whose intellectual abilities run along a spectrum from astoundingly brilliant to unbelievably stupid. It starts to seem a little more like the lottery, only the odds are much worse.

Genius might not exist and might simply be an idea that we like and so believe in. There are two ideas here: someone will find the answer, and it might be me.

LUDWIG WITTGENSTEIN (1889–1951)—PHILOSOPHER

- Ludwig was the youngest of eight children born into a wealthy and cultured Viennese family. The Wittgensteins were often visited by artistic luminaries including Gustav Mahler and Johannes Brahms.

- A school photograph from the Realschule in Linz, Austria, shows teenage Wittgenstein sitting within a few feet of the teenage Adolf Hitler.

- Although a recognized philosophical genius, Wittgenstein published only one book, *Tractatus Logico-Philosophicus*. In it he outlined his groundbreaking philosophy of language and logic, which has significantly influenced the fields of psychology and psychotherapy.

- During World War I, Wittgenstein commanded an Austrian artillery battery. He was taken prisoner by the Italians, who allowed him to correspond with English philosophers from captivity. During World War II, he worked as a hospital porter in London.

- When his father died, Wittgenstein inherited the family fortune. He gave some of it away to Austrian artists and poets including Rainer Maria Rilke.

- Wittgenstein liked to live an ascetic lifestyle and, thinking that his *Tractatus* had solved all philosophical problems, became a primary school teacher and then a monastery gardener for a while. He was eventually lured back to teaching philosophy at Cambridge.

Ensuring the best encyclopedia entry

It's important to consider now how you want to be written up. Your historical footprint can be analyzed according to its parts, its "toes" studied individually. On each of these little piggies the chiropodist of biography will want to find the bunions of narrative. You need to consider origins, childhood, early career, romance, body of work, death.

Baby genius

Having unremarkable origins obviously doesn't mean you can't be a genius. Behind the gray net curtains of the suburban bungalow lurk many quiet boys and girls waiting for the fated opportunity that will carry them and their intellects away to more fertile ground. However, if you do have a boring background, the two most popular angles are the "hot-housed by zealous parents" or the "left to own devices" ones. Any television dramas made about you will appreciate this opportunity for a montage.

And then one day . . .

It's good to have an epiphanic childhood moment, when you realize what it is you want to do with that monumental talent of yours. Give it some setting. You might be up on a hill or at a cliff's edge or clinging to the spire of some gothic cathedral, somewhere high up, a nice godlike perch.

Crowds can work. The awesome scale of the blood-soaked battlefield makes a dramatic setting. But the childhood moment itself is basically all about lone discovery. If you must have other people present, keep it simple. The repeated rebukes of the memorable mentor or the dying words of the crazed beggar are often more resonant to the historian than the carnage of conquest over some now-abandoned city-state east of Persia—because they are simply simpler.

Extremity please

Extremity is best if you want to make it count with the biographers. They'll enjoy writing about your meetings with the emperor and your rapid rise through the court hierarchy or your soul-searching solitude in urban penury—leaky roofs, consumptive coughs, and all.

The matter of the heart

A turbulent romantic life is a great way to make a mark. Torrid affairs, bastard children, and domestic chaos give you the human factor. Everybody loves a rough diamond. The comforting narrative here is that brilliance and moral rectitude don't go hand in hand, so allowing Mr. and Mrs. Public to think either that in some way the great are no better than them, or that in some way they are disgustingly and intriguingly worse.

Be careful, though. Some "romantic practices" might see you remembered not for your greatness but for your weirdness.

Your Nobel speech

The following is a cut-out-and-keep speech template for when you win your Nobel Prize. Simply cross out the options you don't want and you're good to go.

"Ladies and gentlemen of the Academy, let me first thank you from the bottom of my heart for the great honor you bestow upon me. That I stand before you here today is all thanks to . . .

    a) God

    b) the collaboration and encouragement of colleagues

    c) the support of my lovely wife/partner and my family

    d) my own efforts

As a small . . .

    a) boy

    b) girl

I was always fascinated by . . .

    a) physics

    b) chemistry

    c) medicine

    d) literature

    e) peace

I would wander about my hometown, thinking about . . .

    a) how light traveled

    b) what air was made of

c) why I had a headache

d) whether words could describe what I could see

e) how peaceful it was

They were formative days and filled me with a determination to . . .

    a) understand the universe

    b) get a chemistry set

    c) experiment with drugs

    d) learn to read

    e) live a quiet life

My life since then has been full of . . .

    a) misery

    b) joy

    c) opportunity

    d) difficulties

Achieving recognition for . . .

    a) discovering a theoretical particle

    b) creating a brand-new pollutant

    c) synthesizing a new drug that cures acne/greed/embarrassment

    d) writing a novel about social injustice/globalization/love in spite of a cultural divide/my own sex life

    e) bringing lasting peace to the Middle East

. . . is a dream come true. And having arrived at this exalted status, I feel qualified to offer . . .

    a) some advice

    b) a warning

. . . to those aspiring to greatness in . . .

    a) physics

    b) chemistry

    c) medicine

    d) literature

    e) peace

What you will undoubtedly need most is . . .

    a) determination

    b) luck

    c) wealthy parents

    d) a beard

In conclusion, I believe fundamentally that it is the role of the . . .

    a) scientist

    b) megalomaniac

    c) writer

    d) redundant politician

. . . to make the world a more . . .

    a) physical

    b) chemical

    c) medicated

    d) wordy

    e) mellow

. . . place. Thank you."

CHAPTER ELEVEN

Best in Show

"I am the greatest."

Muhammad Ali

BEST IN SHOW

SO WHO ARE THE BEST GENIUSES? AND WHO IS THE GENIUS'S GENIUS? IT'S TIME TO GET COMPARATIVE AND SUPERLATIVE. YOU CAN MEASURE GENIUS BY THE SIMPLE IQ TEST, OR YOU CAN LOOK AT THE PROFUNDITY OF WHATEVER IT IS YOUR GENIUS HAS DONE FOR THE CONSCIOUSNESSES OF HUMANITY. GENIUS IS A HUMAN QUALITY, SO YOU CAN'T EXPECT NICE, NEAT ANSWERS.

IQ, UQ, we all Q

The student of genius is presented with some particular problems when considering how the great ones are measured and categorized. Let's look at IQ.

Dr. Catharine Morris Cox carried out some possibly unreliable research in 1926 to reveal how the fields of genius pan out in terms of IQ. So who are the big bosses of the G-word? Well, the lauded leaders of lofty intellect are not politicians, they're not scientists, they're not artists—they're philosophers. Yes, philosophers. By all sorts of questionable number crunching they come out with an average IQ of 160.

Oddly, the upper echelons of Cox's flight of researching fancy are not the household names you might expect. Who is the daddy of geniuses? Top dog is Johann Wolfgang von Goethe (210). You know, Goethe. Surely not that many days of your life pass between the conversational quoting of a couple of lines from Goethe's satanic closet drama, *Faust*.

Goethe was a writer and, on average, writers come down the list a bit. So what did Goethe do for humanity with his gargantuan IQ? Well, he was certainly a genius. Somewhat polymathic, Goethe was a little bit scientist, a little bit politician, but mostly poet and dramatist. (He was also nutty enough to attack Newton's ideas on optics and suggest that Napoléon Bonaparte was the savior of European civilization— the joke here is his thinking that European civilization could be saved.) He even discovered the intermaxillary jawbone. In Germany he is rightly revered. But writers suffer from the great tribal difference that we call language. For the average non-German, it's easier to understand the genius of Rembrandt or Beethoven or even Einstein, because the problem of language doesn't intervene. Genius isn't always international.

Are you on the list?

The Morris Cox list has philosophers top, followed by scientists, writers, statesmen, musicians, artists, and, last and least, soldiers. But the samples are different sizes, classical antiquity doesn't get a look in, and the whole thing is a sort of exercise in saying, "Yes, geniuses are clever." And the top flight tends to be polymaths, so the categories seem a bit blurred. That said, we all like a list. Goethe is followed by Emmanuel Swedenborg (scientist and philosopher), Gottfried Leibniz (rationalist philosopher, mathematician, and politician), John Stuart Mill (liberal philosopher and political economist), and Blaise Pascal (mathematician, scientist, and philosopher).

If you should feel disappointed by this top five, that's understandable. No artists, no musicians, no statesmen. It's a bit European, a bit Protestant, a bit male. Somehow the list doesn't satisfy. Thomas Chatterton and Sofia Kovalevskaya above Mozart and Copernicus? It's not a list to please the people.

IQ gives you a number. Goethe was 210, Einstein was a lowly 160! But what good is a number, really?

TOP 10 IQ CLUB

- **210** Johann Wolfgang von Goethe (1749–1832) German polymath (or know-it-all).

- **205** Emanuel Swedenborg (1688–1772) Swedish scientist, philosopher, mystic, and theologian.

- **205** Gottfried Wilhelm von Leibniz (1646–1716) German polymath. Another know-it-all.

- **200** John Stuart Mill (1806–1873) British philosopher and political economist.

- **195** Blaise Pascal (1623–1662) French mathematician, physicist, and religious philosopher.

- **190** Ludwig Wittgenstein (1889–1951) Austrian philosopher.

- **187** Bobby Fischer (1943–) U.S.-born Icelandic chess International Grandmaster and World Chess Champion.

- **185** Galileo Galilei (1564–1642) Italian physicist, astronomer, astrologer, philosopher. And heretic.

- **185** René Descartes (1596–1650) Founder of Modern Philosophy and Father of Modern Mathematics.

- **180** Madame de Staël (1766–1817) Swiss author. Also known as Anne Louise Germaine de Staël.

The unsolvable equation

So is any of this league table stuff any help? The arts and sciences all build on previous knowledge and attainment. They are using tools developed by others. Intellectual superstar and inventor par excellence, da Vinci was never going to invent the lightbulb because the conceptual and material means weren't there to do it. If Shakespeare were alive today, as people like to say, he would write differently because the English language has changed syntactically, semantically, colloquially. So part of his genius is no longer available for use. People don't expect modern literary geniuses to write in the Elizabethan style. Comparisons just don't work—x does not equal y.

"You could always tell she was a genius"

If you are a genius, rest assured people will talk about you. So one very vague way of measuring the importance of geniuses is to see what others say about them.

The author Henry James said of fellow author Rudyard Kipling that he "strikes me personally as the most complete man of genius (as distinct from fine intelligence) that I have ever known." (Ah, those parentheses. James could really do parentheses.) A pretty neat statement for Kipling to cut and paste into his resume.

"Who said what about whom?" quick quiz

1. "For all his kindness, sociability, and love of humanity, he was nevertheless totally detached from his environment and the human beings included in it."
   a) Max Born about Albert Einstein
   b) Claude Monet about Titian
   c) Federico García Lorca about George Bernard Shaw

2. "No, I have not read him—he is far too profound for me."
   a) Ludwig Wittgenstein about Søren Kierkegaard
   b) John Stuart Mill about David Hume
   c) Arthur Miller about Henry Miller

3. "Keep an eye on him. One day he will give the world something to talk about."
   a) Wolfgang Mozart about Ludwig van Beethoven
   b) Robert Greene about William Shakespeare
   c) Henri Matisse about Jackson Pollock

4. "There was things which he stretched, but mainly he told the truth."
   a) Huckleberry Finn about Mark Twain
   b) Franklin Roosevelt about Winston Churchill
   c) William Wordsworth about William Blake

The answers, to keep things simple, are all the a)s.

"He changed my life"

"My genius is in my nostrils." —Friedrich Nietzsche

You might want to measure genius by a number of other criteria more favorable to certain wayward intellects. How did genius X affect the way I live? In what ways do his or her ideas shape our thinking? What contribution did the genius make to humanity's understanding of its place in the universe? And so on. All sorts of measurements spring to mind.

This gives inventors and artists a chance. People like Thomas Edison and Nikola Tesla, even Tim Berners-Lee or Bill Gates have had ideas that have developed into the mechanisms and devices that run the modern world. And this is probably a good thing. People like Johann Sebastian Bach and Mahler and Verdi and even Bob Dylan can reflect and influence the way people think and feel. Yes, so did Hitler and Stalin. But don't think of them in the same way. Bach outlives them with sublime ease.

The truth about philosophers

What exactly is it about philosophers that makes them the top geniuses? To paraphrase Plato: "What the hell is a philosopher anyway?" Well, they are the original lovers of wisdom—"*philos*" meaning loving and "*sophos*" meaning the wise. They get into genius territory early because they are the only game in town.

As an early philosopher you could study anything—math, science, astronomy, physics. All these words have their origins in Greek words with rather general senses that mean things like "looking at," "dividing up," "thinking about," "knowing of." If you did any kind of analytical study in the classical world, you were a philosopher.

And the Greeks' achievement is still with us. If you imagine a philosopher today, chances are he'll be sporting a beard, wearing a toga, and carrying a wax tablet, rather than wearing a corduroy jacket and very square glasses, and not knowing what to do with his bicycle clips.

What is truth?

Philosophers want to know what can be known. So they are like ordinary people in that respect. But most people think they know things and just leave it at that. For the philosopher this is not enough.

The philosopher's launch pad is the Socratic method. This means asking questions about things that you normally don't

PLATO (427–347 B.C.E.)—PHILOSOPHER

- Plato was the founder of the Academy in Athens, where Aristotle was a student. The Academy flourished for over 900 years, from 387 B.C.E. to 529 C.E., until it was eventually shut down by Emperor Justinian for being too pagan for the new Christian empire.

- Not too keen on the idea of democracy, Plato instead believed in the rule of philosopher kings.

- The philosopher was originally a wrestler (Plato is a nickname meaning "broad-shouldered") and a soldier in the Peloponnesian War. After the war he joined the government but fell out with

the Thirty Tyrants. Why? Because they were too tyrannical.

- Plato was a student of Socrates and may have attended his trial. He wrote the Socratic dialogues—Socrates himself wrote nothing. Scholars say the later dialogues become increasingly less Socratic and more Platonic.

- *The Republic* is Plato's key text. Written around 360 B.C.E., it sets out his ideas on government, justice, and the role of the philosopher.

- Plato certainly had some nutty moments. Like suggesting that Homer should be exiled and his works rewritten.

ask questions about. Questions like "How do I know I exist?" or "What is the meaning of justice?" or "How can I talk about that which cannot be said?" You do need to exercise caution with these kinds of questions; they can cause trouble. To be a successful philosopher you need to be able to get the questions right as much as the answers.

The 21st-century philosopher

Philosophers these days are still university lecturers—much like Plato was. Though now they don't wear togas or even ties, and they sit in lightless common rooms discussing . . . well, the kinds of things they have always discussed. If they're good they might get to tour universities, delivering "guest lectures," where they become performing artists.

It is hard for philosophers to get the kind of recognition they have historically earned, because our fast-paced, hi-tech, modern societies are quite prepared to bask, pleasured and comforted by the myriad sparkly distractions that rampant capitalist consumerism brings, in philosophical waters so shallow that a toddler could wade in them with little or no concern for its own safety.

The golden days of the professional thinker training up philosopher kings to rule Mediterranean utopias are long gone. A world leader these days is more likely to need a media advisor than a philosopher. Sad but true.

Why I am not a genius

The thing about genius is that you never can tell. By rights I really should have shone through in some exalted field or another. I have an impeccable background, so it's all a bit of a mystery. The signs have always looked pretty auspicious.

I was certainly hot-housed by my father. He employed tutors for me starting when I was only three. As a young child I was given an abacus, a globe, a compass, a geometry set, a chemistry set, and a microscope. All of these objects were magical inspiration dust to my fancy. I made the abacus into a truck, used the globe as a bowling ball with test tubes from the chemistry set as pins, used the compass to persuade my little sister that unless her heart always faced north she would die, and used the geometry set and the microscope to carry out some micro-voodoo on her dolls. I was tutored in music by a Miss Anne Dante, who taught me to play cello like Pablo Casals, piano like Vladimir Horowitz, bassoon like Joseph Holbroke, and cornet like Bix Beiderbecke. She taught my sister to play harmonica like Sonny Boy Williamson. I always felt she didn't really want us to express ourselves. I was tutored in math and divinity by Otto O'Brandt, a fiery and troubled Irish-German Catholic-Protestant. Quite a lot of the math was about probability and we spent a lot of time reading the Racing Post and calculating odds and variables.

At age 14, I was apprenticed to an Italian painter, Tino Bassanini. The first things he taught me were how to drink and visit brothels, but his brushwork was exemplary, and the fact that he was a reckless libertine didn't have much more effect than the occasional six-week absence. The final straw was his failure to appear at my exhibition in Florence, where I showed my best two paintings—*The Day After the Lifting of the Siege of Mafeking* and *The Wreck of the Hesperus II: A Pig's Tale.* I heard later that he could not attend because he was fighting a duel with my father. Whatever happened, Mr. Bassanini was never to reappear and the exhibition was a limited success, so I decided to try academia for a while.

I got into the Sorbonne by becoming a cleaner there. It allowed me to sit in on lots of lectures. After three years or so, aided by a little financial sweetener that Mr. O'Brandt sent from the Cayman Islands, I persuaded a student who was writing a thesis on the modern self to change his name to mine, take some exams, and pick up a degree in the comparative study of the social and cultural effects of scientific theory.

Having got my degree from the Sorbonne, I used the same method to pick up a PhD from Harvard in the comparative study of the scientific effects of social and cultural theory. Then I used these degrees to get a job at the CERN Supercollider in Switzerland. I thought doing some physics and working with a particle accelerator would be pretty cool but I joined during a bit of a slow patch—W and Z bosons had already been discovered and the NA48 experiment into Kaon decay was still a few years away—and I never really took to it. I was planning to leave Switzerland anyway as I wanted to try my hand at being a playwright in London.

Unfortunately, at this time I was associating with the wrong crowd. I got drawn in to taking part in a military coup (see my book *How to Rule the World*). I regret what I did and can only say that I was not focused on being a genius. Once the authorities let me go I quickly went back to my original plan.

Of course, being a playwright is not the kind of job that pays much at first. So, my sister, having just snared herself a wealthy industrialist, was looking for some charitable tax relief. O'Brandt put the package together and I had some cash to set me off. I decided that I wanted to start as strongly as possible and so I re-wrote *Hamlet* by William Shakespeare, giving it a bit more of a musical rom-com angle and setting it in Oklahoma. I wanted the soliloquies to be raps, which is undoubtedly what Shakespeare would do if he were writing today, and was pretty pleased (if I do say so myself) with the big solo number, "What's the Question?", which used some nice phat beats but kept the original iambs "2 bad or not 2 bad, is I or ain't I?" I felt it retained the essence of Shakespeare's play, minus the revenge tragedy bit, but not many theatres wanted to put it on. The part of Hamlet, or Buddy Ham, as I re-titled him, requires an actor of particular sensibilities and the guy I hired turned out to be a psycho. During rehearsal he tried several times to strike me. Reader, I parried him.

While I may go back to exhibiting work in galleries—I recently produced a video installation based on the color puce for a Madrid gallery—my next project is some mathematical research. O'Brandt and my sister's fourth husband, a government minister, have lined me up a consultancy with the ethical statistical analysis department of a Scottish university. It may well be that another Scottish Enlightenment is about to blossom and that my genius will be recognized at last.

WHO'S WHO IN
HOW TO BE A GENIUS

Conceived and produced by
Elwin Street Limited
3rd Floor, 144 Liverpool Road
London N1 1LA

Author: Paul Barker
Illustrator: Robin Chevalier
Designer: Thomas Keenes

ISBN: 978-0-9546309-7-3

Printed in China